DISRUPTING THE GAME

FROM THE BRONX
TO THE TOP OF NINTENDO

REGGIE FILS-AIMÉ

HARPERCOLLINS
LEADERSHIP

AN IMPRINT OF HARPERCOLLINS

Published by HarperCollins Leadership, an imprint of HarperCollins Focus LLC.

Any internet addresses, phone numbers, or company or product information printed in this book are offered as a resource and are not intended in any way to be or to imply an endorsement by HarperCollins Leadership, nor does HarperCollins Leadership vouch for the existence, content, or services of these sites, phone numbers, companies, or products beyond the life of this book.

ISBN 978-1-4002-2668-9 (eBook)

ISBN 978-1-4002-2667-2 (HC)

Library of Congress Cataloging-in-Publication Data

Library of Congress Cataloging-in-Publication application has been submitted. Printed in the United States of America

22 23 24 25 26 LSC 10 9 8 7 6 5 4 3 2 1

To my parents and brother, who gave this kid from the Bronx everything he needed in life, the most important of which was love. To my children, who have guided me as much as I have guided them. And to my wife, Stacey, who has been the best partner I could ever ask for; throughout our life together, she has encouraged me in all my endeavors—including this book.

CONTENTS

PREFACE

I am fortunate to have lived my life at the intersection of capability and opportunity. This is an adaptation of the Roman philosopher Seneca's definition of luck: "a matter of preparation meeting opportunity."

But I wasn't lucky.

I started life as the child of Haitian immigrants and initially lived in a Bronx tenement. Through academic merit, I was able to attend Cornell University on scholarship. I was fortunate to have some excellent jobs and bosses early in my career, and I also had some that were far from excellent. I became president of Nintendo of America and succeeded in that role not through luck but by always making the most of every opportunity.

I was driven to learn by engaging in new experiences and by having an insatiable curiosity. I asked countless questions; I wanted to know stuff, and not just stuff in a narrow field of interest. It wasn't just knowledge for knowledge's sake, but knowledge that I was able to use as a leader and a disrupter. Knowledge helped me come up with innovative solutions to problems that initially appeared unsolvable.

Opportunity came when I saw the potential to achieve in ways that others didn't immediately see. This led me to often choose untraditional paths that ran counter to expectations.

As I progressed in my life and career, I began to group my thinking into core lessons that I valued. For me, these lessons provided a foundation for how to approach a problem or a decision. Shaped by my experience and learning offered by others, they provided a shortcut to help me move forward. Applying these lessons helped keep me and the companies I worked for from making one-off decisions that wouldn't stand the test of time.

In sharing stories from my life and the lessons I learned along the way, I hope to help you add to your own capability. And I hope to challenge you to leap at the opportunities you create, or that are presented to you.

I will present these lessons as "So What"—as in, "so what does this mean and why does this matter?" These are interspersed within my stories, driving home my lessons and giving you actionable advice as you go on your own journey.

DISRUPTING
THE GAME

1

FAREWELL TO MY FRIEND

It was by far the hardest trip I ever had to make. It wasn't because this was the third trip to Japan in less than six months. It wasn't because a nearby typhoon was causing the plane to shake violently throughout the trip.

No, the reason this was my toughest trip was because I was going to Kyoto for the memorial services of my boss, my mentor, and my friend, Nintendo's global president, Satoru Iwata.

Truly, the most troubling part of the flight was knowing that my friend was gone.

There is no way I could prepare for such a trip, beyond educating myself about the protocols for the service: a specific way to walk up to the area for the viewing of the remains, and a specific way to pinch the powdered incense and then raise it to my forehead. I knew that I would be watched closely. I doubted there would be another Black American there. And as the president of Nintendo of America, I always drew attention.

The last time I saw Mr. Iwata was just a few months prior in March 2015. Via email, he had asked me to come back to Japan, right around the time of my birthday. This was odd as I had been in Japan in late January—a typical biannual, one-week visit during which the company's senior leadership discusses our business strategies and our upcoming products. To be summoned back so soon was very unusual.

For this unexpected trip in March, I had asked Mr. Iwata for a bit more detail on the purpose; he was vague. I tried to explain to him that the dates he wanted me to visit with him would interfere with my birthday plans I had with my wife, Stacey, but he would hear none of it. He was adamant that he wanted me there in Kyoto with him for a very specific three-day period.

It was also strange that Mr. Iwata wanted me to be at his office at 8:30 a.m., versus his typical start at nine. The early start made my entrance into the Nintendo Co., Ltd. global headquarters a bit more challenging. With its glass-and-concrete exterior and marble entry, the office felt cold and sterile, especially at the early hour when I arrived. Nintendo, like most Japanese companies, had strict operating hours for most employees. You would hear chimes in the building to signify the start of the workday, and other chimes to signal the start and end of the lunch break. I don't remember hearing chimes at the end of the day—maybe the company didn't believe they needed to remind the staff to go home.

Fortunately, Mr. Iwata's assistant had arrived at the office early, and she was waiting to open the doors for me and help navigate the elevators. To reach the seventh-floor executive area, only a specific elevator could be used, and at that hour it required card-key access.

I was shown to a small conference room that would double as my office during this stay. I took off my overcoat and proceeded to log into the wireless internet system. Nintendo takes its security very seriously, and even as a company executive I was given a unique login and password combination for every visit. I would always arrive early to make sure I was fully connected before the start of my first meeting.

At precisely 8:30 a.m., Mr. Iwata's assistant came for me, and I was ushered to his office.

While Mr. Iwata had been the company's global president for well more than ten years at this point, he had not moved into the formal, large president's office used by his three predecessors. Instead, he had preferred a simpler office, with his desk at the head of a rectangular conference-room setup that could hold up to twelve additional people. In addition to two large television screens that could be used to showcase either presentations or video games in development, Mr. Iwata had cabinets full of books, video games, game accessories, and controllers. It was more of a game creator's office than that of a company president.

After our usual pleasantries, he asked me to sit down, and I studied his face closely. He then told me why he had insisted on my trip. "Reggie," he said, "my cancer is back."

I was shocked. Sure, Mr. Iwata had lost weight from his prior surgery and fight with the disease. But his energy was strong. Just days prior, he had announced a major investment for Nintendo to enter the mobile gaming market. All the signals up to now had suggested he had beaten the cancer. To see his concern, and for him to bring me back to Kyoto specifically to tell me in person, heightened my anxiety, and I focused on every detail he shared.

We talked about his condition and future treatment for quite some time. He shared details about the advanced medical therapeutics he would try. In addition to the high-tech approaches, he told me that his wife was making him special juice and protein drinks to have in the morning and at midday to improve his overall diet. No option seemed too small for him to consider.

After a while, the tone of the conversation changed. Mr. Iwata said: "Reggie, this is just one part of the reason that I wanted you to come to Kyoto. To have this conversation. There are other things we need to discuss. We need to discuss the upcoming launch of our new system. I want you to see the early games and to feel a prototype in your hands. We need to work on the planning because this device will be critical to the future of Nintendo."

This conversational shift was typical for Mr. Iwata; he was prioritizing the business before his own needs. I am sure that, in his mind, now that we had talked about his personal situation, it was time to move on to discussing the business.

For the balance of this visit, we had a series of meetings to discuss all the details for what would later be known as the Nintendo Switch. These meetings were all business, but when Mr. Iwata and I had lunch by ourselves, or when the meetings were finished late in the evening and I was back at the hotel, my mind would return to my friend's illness.

The friendship that Mr. Iwata and I had was deep. Its foundation was mutual respect, as we admired the core capabilities that each of us brought to the company. Mr. Iwata was the brilliant game developer and programmer. He had made personal contributions to many of the greatest franchises in Nintendo's history, including *Pokémon*, *Kirby*, and *Super Smash Bros.*

I was the marketer and business disrupter, integrating consumer insight and commercial knowledge into new initiatives. We trusted and challenged each other at the same time.

The launch advertising for Nintendo's Wii console that I executed for the Americas is a great example. This was in the fall of 2006, after I had been promoted from executive vice president of sales and marketing to president and chief operating officer for Nintendo of America. The advertising featured two Japanese businessmen traversing the Americas and showing off this latest Nintendo innovation, with a focus on the controller: the magical Wii Remote.

Mr. Iwata had stewarded the development of the Wii Remote with the teams in Kyoto. The key innovation was motion-sensing technology that would enable you to move the remote to play a game. Players could swing the remote like a bat in a baseball game or move an arm to swing a racket and play virtual tennis.

The advertising was compelling because we communicated the broad range of game experiences players could have with the Wii

Remote. And we made the ads fun and relatable, with the Japanese businessmen interacting with the families they encountered. The businessmen played a variety of Wii video games with the families, including some that had funny movements and mannerisms. This all took place in an easy camaraderie. Each ad would start with the now famous line, "Wii would like to play."

I championed the advertising developed in partnership with our agency, Leo Burnett, and shared the finished advertising with Mr. Iwata in advance. A week before we were to start running the advertising, Mr. Iwata called me at home. "Reggie, I have been showing the advertising to people here in Kyoto, and there are concerns." The issue for the Nintendo executives back in Japan: our Japanese businessmen in the ads were interacting with the Western families in a manner that was too familiar, too informal. "Reggie, you need to change the advertising."

This issue raised by the teams at Nintendo's headquarters cut at a core, successful element of the advertising. To change this would mean scrapping the work. My advertising experience suggested this was wrong. I knew the advertising was breakthrough and compelling. We proceeded to go back and forth on the issue, and why I thought the "excessive familiarity" was not a concern for our consumers in the US, Canada, and Latin America.

After making little progress, I said, "Mr. Iwata, you brought me to Nintendo because you needed a strong marketer for the biggest Nintendo region in the world. You have seen my performance. You just promoted me. You need to trust me that I know what will work. And I know this advertising will work here in the Americas."

After a pause that seemed eternal, Mr. Iwata said, "Yes, Reggie. I trust you. Please go ahead." The advertising worked, along with a number of other marketing elements my region implemented. We had the best performance for Wii in the world.

THE SO WHAT

There is a fine balance between staying true to your beliefs versus just being stubborn. Do you truly believe in a particular course of action or is it your ego talking? When you are making a difficult or complex judgment, it's especially difficult to know your own motivation.

Be honest with yourself. Separate your own desire to be right or win an argument from your own core beliefs. Can you honestly say that you believe in your recommendation because it's the right thing to do—that you'd get behind it even if someone else suggested it?

When you're unsure how to answer this question, listen carefully and open-mindedly to the alternative perspectives being shared. Ask clarifying questions. Repeat back the issue so the other person knows they are being heard. Demonstrate your understanding of the issue and why the other perspective has value.

If you decide you're being true to your beliefs, present your perspective as persuasively as you can. Use data, examples from other industries, and your own experience to drive the point home. Stop and let others ask you questions. You can't just try to steamroll the other perspective.

Search for common ground. Where there is agreement, state it so that you can focus on the remaining outstanding issues. Sometimes those are minor enough that you can agree to move on.

But sometimes you need to take a stand.

Mr. Iwata and I would have deep conversations about the business. We did not always agree. But throughout the discussion, we would typically get to solutions that worked brilliantly for the company.

It is fair to say that I pushed my point of view. I did this with a combination of persistence and empathy. I believe in the art of business jujitsu, where you push hard on an idea, and gather support, until the idea has a natural momentum that carries it forward.

Mr. Iwata was first diagnosed and had his initial surgery in the summer of 2014. While he was still in the hospital, I was due to be in Japan for our global strategic meetings. Leading up to the trip, I had asked Mr. Iwata if I could visit him. In our back-and-forth emails, he wrote, "No, this just isn't done in Japan. Business associates don't visit the hospital for each other." But I pushed. I explained that after the summer, I was not to be back in Japan for some time, and I wanted to see him. I wanted to understand how he was really doing.

Mr. Iwata continued to push back, and he wrote, "Reggie, no one from the office has come to see me." I challenged the notion that this was a business visit. I wrote back, "With all due respect, Mr. Iwata, I want to visit you not as the president of Nintendo of America but as a friend." I'd like to believe my final push elicited that little smile he would give me when he realized that I just wouldn't take no for an answer. He relented and agreed for me to come visit him in the hospital.

It was a trip that was coordinated by Mr. Shuntaro Furukawa, who would later become the sixth global president of Nintendo. At this point, Mr. Furukawa was the head of corporate strategy and acted as Mr. Iwata's right-hand person in Kyoto. Mr. Furukawa spent years in Europe and spoke fluent English. He was to pick me up from my hotel and direct me to Mr. Iwata's hospital room. On the drive there, Mr. Furukawa reinforced how unusual my visit would be. He shared that until just a few days prior, Mr. Iwata had not allowed any visitors from Nintendo to the hospital. Now that I was due to visit him, he had relented and during the preceding forty-eight hours he had accepted other visitors from the company.

Mr. Iwata was excited about my visit. His wife and daughter would be there as well. This delighted me, since having his family there would make it even more of a friend's personal visit versus a businessman's visit.

Getting to Mr. Iwata's room was very challenging. Kyoto University Hospital was first established in 1899—ten years after Nintendo was founded. The hospital had been renovated many times, including the addition of a ward through the private donations of the Yamauchi family—the founding family of Nintendo. With almost no signage in English, and the labyrinth of hallways from the new wards to older ones, the only way I found the room was because Mr. Furukawa was along to guide me.

As we entered the room, Mr. Iwata was standing in his hospital gown with a big smile on his face. I did what I always did when I saw Mr. Iwata: I shook his hand. We slipped into a very easy and personal conversation about how he was recovering. He looked good. His face had a rosy glow and he radiated good health. His hair was combed in his typical style, parted down the middle. It was a little longer than usual, looking like a Japanese version of John Lennon from the 1960s, complete with the small oval eyeglasses. He introduced me to his petite wife, and he proceeded to do the translation back and forth as she did not speak any English. He also introduced me to his twentysomething daughter. She was very excited that I was there. Mr. Iwata said, "Reggie, she's quite a fan of yours." I said, "Really, Mr. Iwata? I didn't know I had additional fans in your family!"

He chuckled and his daughter and I did some small banter, with Mr. Iwata doing the translating. His daughter took out her cell phone and asked if she could take a selfie with me there in the hospital room. This made Mr. Iwata laugh and he asked me if it would be okay.

I said of course, but there was a problem. I'm a tall man, and his daughter was small; capturing both of us within a selfie frame was proving to be challenging. With a mischievous little smile and twinkle in his eye, Mr. Iwata came to the rescue. He took her phone and proceeded to play photographer, taking several shots of the two of us together, making sure his daughter was happy with the photo.

THE SO WHAT

I believe in the power of personal relationships.

Mr. Iwata wasn't just my boss. He wasn't just someone who valued me for my business acumen. He was a friend, and that friendship made a difference, not just in my success at Nintendo but in my life.

This doesn't mean everyone in business is your friend.

It does mean that the better you understand someone, the more effective you will be in working with them to maximize the results of your work together. By understanding someone's background, perspective, and experience, the better you can solve problems. This is true for boss-subordinate relationships and for peer-to-peer relationships.

In business, you need three types of relationships. You need coaches who have done your work and are able to tell you how to go about the job. Coaches talk to you. You also need mentors who can talk with you. They help with the nuances and can suggest alternative approaches or ideas. Lastly, you need sponsors. They talk about you in a positive way . . . especially when you are not in the room.

In my mind, the happy moment in Mr. Iwata's hospital room is juxtaposed against the funeral that took place about a year later. The funeral itself is ingrained in my memory. When we landed in Tokyo, we had planned to take a short flight onward to Osaka and then a train to the temple where the viewing was being held. This was not typical; usually we would just take the Shinkansen high-speed train into Kyoto. The train ride took a little longer but was more consistent. But we were time pressed as the viewing was being held that evening and the funeral the following day.

There were several of us traveling together representing Nintendo of America. We had changed into our black suits in the bathroom of the plane. That itself was a challenge for a man my size with the plane violently shaking with turbulence from the impending typhoon. The flight attendants asked the other passengers to please let us off the plane first as we were delayed and now our connection would be very tight. We also received expedited help through immigration. But once through immigration, we were informed that our next flight might be delayed or outright canceled. We needed to decide whether to stay with our plan to fly, then train, or to take a Shinkansen directly to Kyoto. The team turned to me. If I made the wrong call, we might not make it to the viewing at all.

I decided we would take the Shinkansen. These trains run exactly on time, with uniformed conductors apologizing for a one-minute delay—or even for arriving early.

By the time the train pulled into Kyoto Station, we were cutting things close. We needed to take taxis to the temple but had to wait in a queue that created further delay. A member of my team had called ahead and asked that the temple stay open for us, but we had no idea if they would accommodate the request.

We finally arrived at our destination. Only a few people remained. We learned that earlier in the day, more than a thousand people attended the viewing. I saw some familiar faces, as Nintendo staff had managed the huge crowds from earlier. Mr. Tatsumi Kimishima was the senior person on-site. Mr. Kimishima had hired me when he was president of Nintendo of America. Now he was Nintendo's chief financial officer and would later become the fifth global president of Nintendo, officially succeeding Mr. Iwata.

Because we were arriving so late, Mr. Iwata's coffin had been covered with a ceremonial cloth in preparation for the funeral the next day. As I gathered myself to go through the protocols I had memorized, Mr. Kimishima asked me if I wanted to see the body of my friend. I said yes.

I stood in front of Mr. Iwata for some time. I had to accept that my friend, my mentor, my guiding force at Nintendo, was gone. It was this, Mr. Iwata's passing, that motivated me to think deeply about my career and to think about the legacy I wanted to leave at Nintendo. And beyond.

2

DICTATORS, DELINQUENTS,
AND BLOOD

A core principle for me is that life is hard, so you need to find strength and determination within yourself to move forward and succeed. When Mr. Iwata died, I was reminded of this valuable principle. But this principle was formed early on.

Until I was eight, I lived in the Bronx. At that age you don't know about other perspectives and situations. You know only about your own reality, and for the four of us in my family it was the reality of living in a one-bedroom, fifth-floor walk-up apartment in a tenement building with roaches and mice.

My parents certainly knew that this was a rough situation. They had come from a life of relative privilege in Haiti where they had grown up. Haiti in the 1940s and 1950s was very different than today. The economy was healthier, a middle and upper class existed, and top-tier education was available to these groups.

During this time, both of my grandfathers had prominent roles within the Haitian government. On my father's side, my grandfather Henri was a senior officer for the Haitian army. I would later hear stories and see pictures of Henri with President Dwight D. Eisenhower when he was visiting Haiti, as well as with senior political and military personnel from other Caribbean islands and Central America. I later learned that he was the second-highest ranking officer in the Haitian military.

He lived in a magnificent home. My father had six siblings, so the building and grounds of the family home were quite large—large enough to be turned into a hotel once the children had grown. The house itself was eggshell-colored, and the wood floors were a shiny mahogany. There was a huge pool, with flowering hibiscus plants circling the outer area. I visited there once at age ten, and I can still hear the chirping of the birds and visualize the exotic plants that I wouldn't see again until visiting other tropical islands as an adult.

On my mother's side, my grandfather Camille was a doctor who had studied at the best schools in Haiti. He had also traveled to Canada and the United States to get additional advanced degrees, including from Harvard. Later, my grandfather would be a professor at Haiti's National Medical School and become the secretary of health and education for the democratic government of Haiti.

He commanded attention: tall, sharp witted, and articulate, speaking perfect Parisian French and English. As a child, I remember his challenging me to read aloud to him, and how he would sternly correct me if I mispronounced a word.

Camille left government service in 1951 after witnessing high-level corruption and refusing to be part of it. He was stripped of his title and jailed for a time to silence him. In 1957, the government would transition to leadership under the brutal dictator François Duvalier.

As Duvalier abused his power and the people of Haiti, my grandfather Camille became even more outspoken. He prepared to go to New York City to speak at a United Nations conference about the situation in Haiti and the troubling path the country was on. Before his departure, he learned that if he left the country and spoke at the UN, he would never be allowed to return. Despite the prospect of exile, he decided that he had to make the trip and speak up. He was a man of principle. His wife, my grandmother Rolande, and their young son, my uncle Jacques, would not be traveling to the US with him and remained in Haiti.

True to Duvalier's threats, once my grandfather left Haiti, he was never allowed to return. And as my grandmother was making plans for her and my uncle to join him in New York City, she was told by the government that she would never be allowed to leave Haiti. She and my uncle would be forced to live in hiding under the protection of friends and family. My grandmother never saw her husband again.

Over the same time during which my maternal grandfather was agitating against Duvalier, my paternal grandfather, Henri, was appointed to serve in Miami's Haitian consulate. My father was about nineteen and joined him at this posting. It was there that my father experienced racism and bigotry for the first time. My father's skin tone was lighter than many Blacks, and he was probably mistaken as Latino or some other nationality. He could not sit in the areas reserved for Whites, nor was he able to be in the area held for Blacks.

He hated his time in Miami, and after a few months he moved to New York City where the Haitian community was growing in Queens, the Bronx, and Brooklyn. There, he reconnected with my mother—they had spent some time together in Haiti at the high society balls and other events when they were teenagers.

They married in 1958 and moved into that tenement building in the Bronx. But the neighborhood was getting worse by the day.

DO THE RIGHT THINGS

Around the ages of six and four, my brother and I would descend the five flights of stairs and walk a couple of blocks to the bodega to get the Sunday *New York Daily News* for our parents. We each had a quarter, and there would be some change left over to buy candy. One Sunday morning, as we were walking toward the bodega, a couple of teenagers blocked our way and demanded our money. In truth, I, and especially my brother, were tough kids, but we were not going to get into a fight with a couple of teenagers. We gave them the money and ran back to our apartment.

My mother was incensed by the robbery. She marched us back to the store. The teenagers were still there. She asked us, "Which ones?" We pointed them out, and they took off. And my mother took off after them. Picture two teenagers running down the street, followed by a thirty-year-old woman, followed by two children. It was a sight.

The teens finally stopped in front of another tenement. Five men in their late twenties and early thirties were hanging out there. The meanest-looking one asked the teens what was going on. One teenager responded that "this crazy-ass woman" was chasing them. My mom said, "Yeah, because you stole money from my boys!" The teens denied it, of course. The man looked at us menacingly and then at the teens. After a beat, he said to the teens, "Gimme the money." Grudgingly, one teen handed over the fifty cents. The man took it and returned it to my mom. We were now five blocks from our building and needed to get the hell out of there. My mother grabbed us by the hands, turned around, and walked away with her head high. She never turned around to look at the group . . . my brother and I sure did. The teenagers were getting a talking-to by the group of men. We returned to the bodega and got the paper for my dad.

THE SO WHAT

Doing what is right, no matter the consequences, should be more than just talk. Pushing back on those doing wrong and driving toward the best outcome should be your constant conduct. My grandfather Camille challenged the dictator Duvalier. My mom confronted the teens who stole our money.

For me, the concept of backing up your beliefs and doing the right things was ingrained at a very young age. The lesson of right and wrong still applies when we're adults.

DIGGING DEEP WHEN LIFE GETS TOUGH

Issues in our Bronx neighborhood finally came to a head one summer Sunday morning. We would often make a family trip to a lake in northern New Jersey. It was a central meeting place for our extended family who lived throughout metropolitan New York City. We would typically be up and out the door by eight o'clock in the morning so we could be assured of getting a good spot at this lake. My father would make a few round trips up and down the five flights of stairs carrying coolers and blankets into the car before my mother, my older brother, and I would head down.

One morning, there was some sort of commotion. When my father came back after making an initial trip to load up the car, he and my mother were having a heated conversation. When it was time to leave, my mother pulled my brother and me aside and told us, "When we are going down the stairs to the car, I want you to do something for me. I want you to look up and not down. Do this for me."

Well, when you're six years old and your mother implores you to do something—something that didn't make a lot of sense as we were preparing to walk down the stairs—what do you do? Of course, you do exactly the opposite!

I looked down as we left the apartment, and it was clear what she didn't want us to see: drops of blood dotting the stairs from the roof, trailing past our door and down the next flight of stairs. As we descended, the drops became dramatically larger and more numerous

. . . expanding from dime to quarter size. By the time we reached the first floor and headed out the doors of the building, we saw a large volume of blood scattered in all directions where people had obviously walked through it. We learned later that a man had been stabbed on the roof the night before and had stumbled down the five flights of stairs bleeding as he made his way outside the building. The man survived, but my parents were now insistent that we move out of the Bronx and give my brother and me a better chance at life.

My father worked two jobs, six days a week. My family saved as much as they could in order to afford a small house in Brentwood, Long Island.

THE SO WHAT

I learned early that opportunity is not simply handed out, like candy at that Bronx bodega. Life is hard and so you must dig deep. Persevere. Demonstrate grit. You take your life experiences and either toughen up or wither away. I got tough. I learned to push for what I wanted. I learned this from my family, and I continue to heed that advice today.

3

GETTING ABOVE
CAYUGA'S WATERS

I flourished in Brentwood. The area was very different in the late 1960s and 1970s versus today. The town had a large population—so large that there were four mini school districts within the larger one, each designated by the main directions on a compass. We lived in North Brentwood. In later grades, North and West Brentwood were combined into one high school. East and South were combined into a different high school. Each high school graduated more than seven hundred students a year.

When I grew up there, the population was largely White. Poverty was low, with both parents typically working. My family stood out. We were the only Black people for blocks. Most kids at our school simply accepted us, but there were some fights as kids tried to push me or my brother around. We were able to take care of ourselves, and later only the most boneheaded—or racist—decided to fight again. Some adults would look at us cautiously, telling their sons or daughters to stay away. But it was much safer than our old Bronx neighborhood.

Academically, students of similar capability were grouped together. I was fortunate to be with other very bright kids. We had access to honors classes beginning in the seventh grade. College-level courses were available to us as juniors and seniors in high school. New York State administered tests at the conclusion of every academic year to assess proficiency in the material. Colleges and universities had access to our scores, and I began receiving college brochures by the end of my freshman year in high school. Good thing, because neither my parents nor the guidance department knew how to help prepare me for life after high school.

My parents understood the school system in Haiti and had graduated with the equivalent of college diplomas but had no exposure to the educational system in the US. They could not help me differentiate state universities from private colleges, let alone the Ivy League schools.

APPLYING MYSELF

The guidance department at the high school was overwhelmed. There were no more than a couple of counselors supporting seven hundred juniors and seven hundred seniors. Students received only generic information: these schools are good, these ones are easy to get into. Not only was I on my own when it came to choosing a school, but I also had to figure out the application process by myself.

In the late 1970s, no common college application existed. Each school had its own materials. You either wrote out the application by hand or used a typewriter to fill in the blanks. Either approach was time consuming.

Each application also had a fee. I don't remember the amount, or the cost to provide each college access to your standardized test scores. But at the time, $25 per application felt like $250 per application. I could not afford to take a scattershot approach.

The other challenge would be how to pay for my education. My parents had little savings. They would not be able to take out loans. I would be solely responsible for my college fees, making cost a major criterion in selecting where to apply.

A good high school friend was looking into ROTC to fund his college tuition, and it motivated me to investigate this possibility too. Army, Navy, and Air Force all offered ROTC scholarships. Each had programs at top-tier universities. Scholarships paid full tuition, rooming costs, textbooks, and a monthly stipend. The first two years came with no service commitment. But beginning the third year, you had an active-duty military commitment. A difficult choice would be looming the summer between sophomore and junior year of college if I took this path.

PLAYING GAMES: COMPETING FOR FUN AND FOR SCHOLARSHIPS

I had another avenue to help pay for college—an athletic scholarship. I played a variety of sports growing up. My passion was basketball. My parents put a hoop up in our driveway, and I would shoot for hours. Rain did not make me stop. I shoveled our driveway in the winter so I could keep practicing. I tried out for our school team beginning in the seventh grade. I did not make it that year . . . I was one of the last players cut. That just made me work harder.

I also played soccer. This was the passion sport of my father, and we spent time watching games together as I grew up. I was exposed to the World Cup before I learned of March Madness. As a big guy with lateral speed, I was a natural defender.

Sports was an avenue for me to unleash my competitiveness and drive. My friends all played sports and were good students; this combination of interests and intelligence bound us together in a small, loyal group. In addition to physical sports, we played all types of games, including video games. It was with this group that I played on Magnavox Odyssey, Atari, and Coleco systems. Video games were something to play as we hung out together.

I played soccer in the fall, basketball during the winter, and for fun participated in track and field during the spring. I competed in a variety of events including shot put, discus, long jump, triple jump, and middle-distance runs. It was a unique combination of strength and speed events. Mainly I did this to stay in shape for the other two sports. But I would win a few events and lettered across all three sports.

I was a good enough athlete that I was generating some interest at the college level. Not with Division I schools, but with smaller Division III programs. I received letters from a variety of schools touting their programs and asking me to fill out questionnaires. The former coach of my high school basketball team was now a college coach, and he ran a basketball camp that I attended. These were all nice strokes for my ego, but I knew deep down that I was not an elite-level athlete. I was more likely to get into college through my brain than my legs.

THE DREAM SCHOOL

In the end, I applied to three schools. Syracuse University was my safe choice. I knew I would be accepted, and the school had several strong programs that interested me. Hobart College also made my list, as they fielded a competitive men's soccer program and were considering offering me a scholarship.

My dream school was Cornell University. As an Ivy League institution, it offered the best academics. They had ROTC programs, so if I received that scholarship, my first two years would be fully funded. Cornell also had an interesting history as a land-grant university. Enacted in the late 1860s, this program offered in-state students a reduced tuition in certain colleges within the university. My undergraduate business program was within one of these colleges, and this made Cornell affordable should I opt out of ROTC as a junior.

THE SO WHAT

Looking back, I realize I had used a methodology that I would apply to a range of challenges throughout my career.

I began by identifying the fundamental objective: how to afford a stellar college education. Being crystal clear in defining the objective would be a hallmark of my business approach.

Before every meeting as a senior executive, I would make sure we articulated both the meeting objective and the ultimate decision we were evaluating. If it wasn't clear, I would interrupt the process to ask the questions: What is our objective? Why are we here?

Without a clear objective, it's difficult to identify the best path to achieve it. Many organizations today are too reactive—they seize on an opportunity or fixate on a problem without stepping back and articulating the ultimate goal.

Once the objective was clear, I tested alternatives and explored options. I developed a plan, with different "what if" scenarios that led to a successful outcome. This sounds like a coldly analytical decision-making process. But I infused my process with emotional awareness and immediacy: if it felt right and strategically fit the objective, I paid attention to this feeling. Finally, I wasn't afraid of making the decision. Once made, I moved on.

I was accepted by all three schools. All offered financial aid. I also received an Air Force ROTC scholarship. I chose Cornell and set foot on campus for the first time to move into my dorm. This is one of a handful of decisions that would define the rest of my life.

INTELLECTUAL CURIOSITY MEETS
PRACTICAL REALITIES

As part of the orientation process for Air Force ROTC before officially starting classes, I had to create my full, four-year schedule of
courses at Cornell and share it with my academic advisor. At the
time, the class registration process was manual. You would pick up
a two-inch-thick Courses of Study book with tiny print that listed
every single undergraduate and graduate class on Cornell's Ithaca
campus. Each included a course synopsis, the name of the instruct-
ing professor, and the necessary prerequisites to attend the class.
With no more information than this, I had to map out my four-year
academic journey.

I dutifully filled out my schedule. The first few semesters carried
reasonable class loads of about fifteen credits per semester. But as I
spent time with that manual of courses, I found classes that piqued
my curiosity. Oceanography. Our Home in the Universe. Monsters
and Mythology. Science, Technology, and Social Change. Introduction to Wine and Spirits. I added these and other classes to my
necessary coursework to graduate with a concentration in business
management and finance. According to this plan, I would be taking
close to twenty credits each semester during my junior year. For my
senior year, it was almost twenty-five credits per semester.

I reviewed this plan with Professor Bruce Anderson, my academic
advisor. His teaching focus was finance and accounting, and his
research focus was business cooperatives. He and I hit it off quickly.
He had done extensive fieldwork throughout the Caribbean and
Africa. This gave him an affinity for my Haitian culture and family
background. He also had a very dry sense of humor. "Reggie," he
said, "most seniors will be wanting to take it easy in their final year.
Why are you proposing a course load in your senior year that would
represent two years of study for most people?"

I explained that Cornell was a once-in-a-lifetime opportunity for me and that I sought classes that were both intellectually challenging but also fun. He shook his head and chuckled, suggested a few small edits to my plan, with a focus on the courses to take in my freshman year. "Let's start here and see how this experiment goes."

Needless to say, I never did take fifty credits' worth of classes my senior year. But the ROTC assignment did force me to think about my Cornell education and to create a plan for how I wanted my four years to unfold.

PIVOTING FROM ROTC TO TA

The ROTC assignment also gave me exposure to two professors who would play critical roles in my time at Cornell: Professor Anderson and Professor Richard "Doc" Aplin. Doc Aplin taught business strategy and did fieldwork on capital allocation and the dairy industry.

After two years in the Air Force ROTC program, I had to make the decision whether to continue with the scholarship and begin to have a military commitment, or to opt out. I took my typical analytic approach to this question and studied what potential Air Force jobs would be available to me. I suffer from poor eyesight, so flying was not an option. With an undergraduate business degree, I would be in the procurement area. I would likely be buying spare airplane parts to start, maybe eventually being a member of the team evaluating fighter planes. But as I looked further into the career path, it struck me as regimented and slow. This would not be the first time that I decided against a regimented and slow path.

I opted out of ROTC but needed a plan to pay for Cornell. I would take out student loans, receive a few small academic scholarships, and fund the balance through work—both during the summer and during the school year.

This is where my relationship with Professors Anderson and Aplin would pay dividends. I worked for each of them, first as a grader for their classes and then as a teaching assistant organizing the graders and class logistics. More than the income, this gave me great exposure to how they approached teaching. I would watch how they reinvented their material every year to keep the content interesting. I observed their meticulous preparation. I also was exposed to coaching others: coaching the students during office hours and coaching/mentoring the other graders as I grew into a position of accountability for their performance.

RECRUITED: THE P&G PATH

I did not know it at the time, but my exposure to key professors within the undergraduate business program at Cornell would lead to a career-defining opportunity with Procter & Gamble.

P&G had a massive recruiting effort focused on Cornell. Every discipline within the company actively recruited—engineering, finance, sales, and brand management. Brand management was the general management function within P&G. Here you learned all the aspects of running a business, including advertising, promotion, pricing, and product development. As you grew within this function, you would gain responsibility for managing people. Just about all the senior positions within the company were filled with executives from this function. And throughout the 1970s, 1980s, and 1990s, many Fortune 500 companies were headed by executives with experience in this functional area from P&G and similar consumer packaged-goods companies.

The recruiting process for brand management was very different than for the other P&G functions. Almost all the candidates had an MBA, so recruiters focused on Cornell's Johnson School of

Management. That interview schedule filled up quickly, and P&G would typically have five or six executives staffing that interview load.

As an undergraduate, the only way to get on the interview schedule was through the personal recommendation of key professors. Fewer than ten undergraduate candidates would be interviewed. And the company contacted you directly, outside of the typical on-campus sign-up process. It was all done very quietly.

To this day, I don't know who lobbied to get me on the P&G interview schedule. I had been singularly focused on a career in banking at the time. I had interned at a bank in between my junior and senior years. I loved the analytical nature of finance. I had envisioned a two- to three-year start at a banking institution and then another two years of education to get my MBA. My dream was to work internationally, leveraging my passion for growing businesses and organizations. I was so focused on this plan that I had not put any effort into alternatives.

I was shocked to get the invitation to interview with P&G. But as I researched the company, I was intrigued by what I learned. The concept of learning to run a business was compelling. Being exposed to all the facets of a business and doing this within a world-class institution was a unique opportunity. Just as my time at Cornell was life changing, this opportunity could be as well.

As I prepared to graduate, P&G offered the opportunity to fast-track my career. I would not have to spend two or three meaningless years in a bank rotation program, only to then spend two more years getting my MBA.

If I was successful, I would be a brand manager at twenty-five and an executive by thirty. If I wasn't successful, I would lose nothing—not even any time. I would leverage the P&G experience and then go to business school, get that MBA, and get back on my original plan of banking.

THE SO WHAT

That I got the job offer from P&G and started my career with them isn't the key learning here. That I was one of a handful of undergrads hired nationally that year to go into this prestigious program isn't the payoff either.

The takeaway: be open to alternative paths and outcomes. Too often we get fixated on only one plan or one solution. You believe that P&G, Apple, Disney, or Google are the only organizations where you'll be happy. Or you're convinced that you want to be in finance or tech and ignore opportunities in other fields. This experience taught me that while you always should have a plan, you need to test it constantly to make sure it is still relevant given the current circumstances.

Being open to alternative plans and outcomes helped me find a great first job consistent with my long-term objective.

4

A BRAND-NEW MANAGER

Every organization has a culture. Culture defines how people act, even when no one is looking. Culture defines how people get ahead. Culture is the air around the place that you breathe every day.

To me, the culture at Procter & Gamble consisted of the one-page memo, the "What Counts" Factors, and "up or out," all of which I'm about to discuss.

THE VALUE OF A PERFECT MEMO

Everything at P&G moved forward based on ideas or initiatives distilled on one piece of paper. From your first day, you were challenged to write clearly and persuasively. Typically, you were working on two or three memos at a time, with a goal of publishing at least one per week to the next level of management. You would share these memos with your boss, and they would come back with more handwritten critique than what was initially typewritten on the page.

You learned to start with a clear articulation of the purpose of the memo. This was another reinforcement to be clear in your objective. Was this a recommendation to launch a new advertisement? Was it a summary of research? Was it a proposal for a reduction in pricing? You needed to be clear at the outset.

Another element of the one-page memo was to frame thinking into threes. Three reasons why your idea made sense. Three key findings from a research report. Always three. I remember asking why, and the answer was put simply: one or two is not convincing enough; four or more is overkill. Three was judged to be the perfect number. I still tend to talk in threes.

An effective one-page memo anticipated concerns about the proposal and rebutted these concerns by stating the risks in pursuing the initiative, and how those risks could be mitigated.

The final element in the perfect one-page memo was clarity on the next steps. This required discipline to fully consider how the initiative could be implemented. For example, if the proposal was to produce a new advertisement, you needed to have already worked to understand the production company to be used and their availability, how many days of filming would be required, how many days to edit, and finally when all the internal approvals would be in hand to have the finished ad ready to run. This drove an attention to detail and an anticipation of what issues would affect the cost and the timetable.

For a twenty-two-year-old fresh out of Cornell, there were two big outcomes from perfecting the one-page memo. The first was strong business writing skills. It would be a point of pride to create a document, deliver it to my boss, and have it sent on to the next level of management without any edits or comments. Admittedly, it would take me months to get to this point. But it felt great when it happened.

The second and bigger outcome was the clarity of thinking that results from laboring over the perfect one-page memo. You learn to assess the big picture and what you are trying to accomplish. You learn to be persuasive. You learn to look for data or external examples to support your proposals. You anticipate questions and have answers ready. You create a detailed action plan to implement your proposal.

FIVE VALUED BEHAVIORS

P&G's "What Counts" Factors defined the behaviors that were valued within the company. The company constantly labors over these factors to make them clear because they are openly shared with every new brand-management employee. They evolve over time, as the business evolves. During my time at the company, there were five "What Counts" Factors:

- *Superb thinking skills.* The focus was on strategy, analytics, and creativity.
- *Personal initiative.* Colloquially, this translated to making things happen.
- *Consumer-led innovation.* You needed to focus on what consumers wanted and figure out how to give it to them while delivering a profit.
- *Creating business-building advertising.* You needed to lead outside entities, such as the advertising agency or production company, in a creative and collaborative process.
- *Developing people and teams.* This was critical because at the time, P&G promoted only from within. As a people manager, you needed to create a pipeline of great people in your footsteps so that you could be promoted.

This final factor was dual edged. As a people manager, you needed to train and develop your subordinates to the best of their abilities. But if they (or you) were unable to get to the next level within the company, it was made clear that you needed to leave. This was the "up or out" element of P&G. Everyone felt this pressure. In fact, within months of joining the company, you would start to get calls from executive recruiters who built successful careers helping P&Gers transition out of the company when it was their time to go.

The message to get out could be overt. During my career, I told a few people they did not have the skills or capacity to get to the next level and that their best next step was to look outside the company. Or it could be more subtle, as others with similar tenure were promoted and you were not. This situation was difficult to manage, as sometimes the company really wanted you to stay but your own impatience, and the constant calls from recruiters, were driving you to look at opportunities with other companies.

THE SO WHAT

Culture and fit can often be overlooked when evaluating a business opportunity. Understand the foundational elements that drive how employees approach situations and how they behave toward one another.

As a junior employee, ask the tough question: "How will I fit into this culture?" In my experience, a bad hire wasn't because the individual didn't have the necessary skills; it was a lack of behavioral fit.

As a senior executive, your challenge is even greater: What parts of the existing culture are positive? Which parts are not and need to be changed? No culture is perfect. And if you don't evolve with emerging business conditions, your company and its culture will be left behind. The best senior leaders define the culture in their organization thoughtfully.

LESSONS IN MENTORING

I was fortunate at P&G to have a great mentor who helped me navigate the culture. His name was Bob Gill, and when I first met him, he was an associate advertising manager, the next level above a brand manager. Bob led the recruiting effort at Cornell. He offered me the job and pressured me to take it when I initially demurred because the competing financial job offers were at a higher salary. He was the first to see my tough Bronx nature as I successfully negotiated an increase in the P&G offer.

It's funny to think about it now: when we were having this intense verbal negotiation, he pulled out a penknife from his desk drawer and began to play with it. Bob must have thought this would intimidate me. But I had been in and seen situations much worse than this. I just chuckled and pushed him to increase my offer. I later learned that a revised offer almost never happens, and certainly not with undergrad salaries. I would work within his organization for five of my eight years at the company.

During one of those brief periods outside Bob's organization, I was getting frustrated that I had not yet been promoted to brand manager. I had seen others hired the same year get promoted, and I believed my list of accomplishments was superior. And I was on the radar of a few recruiters who were tempting me with brand manager jobs outside of P&G at significantly higher salaries. This was the "up or out" clock ticking.

I ended up taking a sick day to visit one of these outside companies. The visit was arranged so that I had a late dinner the evening before the day of interviews where I could be judged in a casual setting. The next day was meeting progressively senior executives. By the end of the day, I had a job offer in hand.

Bob had my office and home numbers, and he had left messages for me on both during my sick day. In retrospect, I was transparent. I had never taken a sick day before in my three-plus years with the company, and this sick day happened to be on a Friday.

I called him back late when I had returned home, and he insisted that I meet him at his house the following day, Saturday. This was very unusual, and I was a little nervous given I had taken a day off to explore another job opportunity.

Bob's house was not at all what I expected. It was an old home that was in the process of being demolished so that he could build his new home using the foundation and other salvageable portions. He was alone at the property, swinging a sledgehammer at drywall. It was a little comical. Bob was in his late forties and had a bad back from playing collegiate football. He was smaller than I, and I didn't think he could swing the sledgehammer very hard for very long. Luckily, I was casually dressed, and he pointed to a spare sledgehammer and invited me to help him as we talked.

Bob told me he was aware that I had been out sick the day before. In fact, he told me that quite a few levels of P&G management were aware that I had been out.

"Reggie, we know you went on an interview yesterday. Next time, do it in the middle of the week, or when you have an already-planned vacation.

"I asked you to come here not to tell you that you screwed up with this masquerade but to tell you to be patient. The company loves you. You have a future here. But you need to be patient."

"Bob," I said, "it's tough to be patient when I see other people being promoted that have done less than I have. And I don't think my current boss is trying to help me." This was a new boss. My prior manager had just taken maternity leave. She had been a great teacher, and I knew she was a sponsor for me. But with her now gone, I felt I had no support.

"Reggie, you have many sponsors in the company. You just need to be patient. The right opportunity will come along, and if you decline that outside job offer you will be happier and better positioned career-wise to become a brand manager here at P&G."

Bob did all the things you want a mentor to do. He was straight with me. No BS. And he gave me real advice: Reaching brand manager at P&G was my ticket. I would never need an MBA or any other credential to get ahead.

THE SO WHAT

Some organizations assign employees a more experienced individual to be a sounding board and a coach. I did this at Nintendo and called these people "mentors." But this was an improper use of the term.

Real mentorship relationships happen over time and naturally—they are not assigned. The relationship is based on a mutual desire for the less experienced employee to do well and grow. Mentors guide and provide perspective; they typically do not tell you what to do. Mentors need not have the same functional background as you, nor must they be in your reporting line. But they should have a strong understanding of your business culture to provide useful perspective.

OUT OF THE BOX

Within weeks, I was told I was being promoted. In fact, I was being promoted into Bob's division. He was now an advertising manager, the senior-most marketing position, for an entrepreneurial group within P&G that was competing in the soft-drink business against Coca-Cola and Pepsi with the Crush, Hires, and Sun Drop brands. It was in this business that I learned how much I loved fast-paced categories. Bob also taught me the power of mentorship, and the difference a mentor can make.

I learned another important lesson as part of this business. After I had been a brand manager for about a year, I had an entry-level position open on my team. Throughout my entire tenure at P&G, I had been involved in the company's recruiting efforts back at Cornell. I had done everything from screening résumés to holding meetings with professors to get recommendations and background on candidates. For the previous two years, I had been part of the team interviewing candidates on campus, as well as interviewing candidates making trips to P&G's headquarters. I had a very good sense for the experiences that enabled candidates to be successful brand managers.

My job opening, though, was outside the typical recruiting cycle. The position opened up in the early fall, and I couldn't wait until the following summer to fill the role with a spring graduate. I worked with HR to get access to applicant résumés who had just missed getting a job offer in the previous cycle, as well as candidates who had sent in their résumés directly to the company. From this, I created the candidate pool and performed phone interviews. I culled the pool to a short list of three candidates I wanted to come to our offices and reviewed this with my direct boss. He reported to Bob.

In my pool I had a nontraditional candidate. Like me, she had only a bachelor's degree; all the other candidates had an MBA. She was not currently working in a marketing role; in fact, she was working as an executive recruiter filling sales-oriented positions at the time. But what I saw in her résumé and during the screening call was an individual who had bootstrapped her way through school and had tremendous personal initiative. She reminded me of me.

My boss zeroed in on this candidate. "Why is she in the mix?" he demanded.

"I like her background. And she answered my questions thoughtfully. I love that she put herself through school and is working now. I see someone hungry to learn and driven to be successful."

My boss grudgingly relented, and we brought in all three candidates. At the end of the process, he and I disagreed on who we should offer the job. He liked a traditional candidate: male, from a big-name school, with an MBA. I liked my nontraditional candidate, Dina

Howell. We argued back and forth. "Reggie, you don't have time to waste. You need someone we have confidence in to do the current job, and to progress within the company," he said.

I stuck to my rationale. "This person is going to work for me. I need to trust my instincts and go with the candidate that has the best near- and long-term potential. Dina is a winner, and she will hit the ground running. I want to hire her."

I give my boss a lot of credit for relenting in the end. I hired Dina, and she performed. In fact, she ended up having a very successful twenty-plus-year career at P&G, surpassing my and my boss's careers there. I wish I could say that I was just prescient. Instead, I placed a higher value on the unique skills and experiences that Dina brought to the company. We had MBA candidates from big-name schools by the hundreds. We didn't have enough people with strong internal drive and personal experiences that provided new points of view.

This was my first real experience as a manager recognizing the value of diverse perspectives and backgrounds. And I never forgot this lesson.

THE SO WHAT

Unfortunately, many give lip service to the concepts of diversity and inclusion but confuse the two and fail to implement them effectively. These are two different but related ideas.

Diversity is the recognition that we are unique in our combination of physical attributes and our life experiences. Each of these differences matters because they help provide unique perspectives for problem-solving.

Diverse perspectives, versus a homogeneous group, will bring forward a broader range of potential solutions and more "out of the box" thinking.

Inclusion is proactively bringing a diverse population together—whether a community or business organization—and enabling these differences to coalesce in a positive way. Making a diverse group feel welcome and valued is the essence of inclusion.

True leaders passionately believe in diversity as a personal and professional imperative and take action. They leverage diversity to drive better results, then they create a culture of inclusion.

OVERSTEPPING MY AUTHORITY

My time in the soft-drink business came to an end about a year later. P&G decided that they wanted to get out of the business and put it up for sale. A few others from the business and I toyed with making a bid for one of the brands: Sun Drop. Sun Drop is a Mountain Dew competitor sold in a handful of states in the South and Midwest. In its markets, it sells on par with Coke and Pepsi. I knew the brand well and had relationships with all the local distributors and retailers.

Once again, my mentor Bob pulled me aside. "Reggie, you are not ready to negotiate with private equity or venture capital people and do a deal like this. But you are close to getting another promotion here. Let this go and stay at P&G a little longer."

At the time, this was a difficult decision for me. While the private equity and venture capital worlds were unknown to me, I was already getting frustrated with the low-growth world of P&G products. If you grew your brand 3 to 4 percent per year, you were a hero. I had been fortunate to work on businesses growing more than 15 percent with Bob's leadership.

I was told I would be going back to work on Crisco shortening, a brand I had worked on years before. Unfortunately, I would be outside of Bob's organization. In the intervening time, the Crisco business had shrunk. It was still highly profitable, but I was not very excited to work on this dying business. Nevertheless, I listened to Bob and let the Sun Drop opportunity pass.

The upside to going back to the Crisco brand was that I knew the fundamentals of the business. I was able to make an immediate impact. The existing staff were good, and under my direction delivered even better results. The best part was that I already had a strong relationship with the advertising agency, and they had just created a new campaign for the brand. The advertising had no words—heresy at the time—and showed the close-up hands of a woman creating a pie using Crisco to make the crust. The visuals were scored to Vivaldi's *Four Seasons*. It communicated strong emotional benefits to mom, and the food photography was world class.

Before my rejoining Crisco, the team had experimented by ending the commercial with a direct response offer providing free recipes to consumers who called an 800 number. There was a significant need to teach consumers to bake and cook with Crisco, and once consumers used a recipe that their family loved, they would never substitute ingredients.

With my rejoining the Crisco team, we took this direct response marketing to the next level. We analyzed the markets where consumers ordered the recipes and tracked growth in the purchase of Crisco. We also used the response data to improve the media plan, running more ads in the shows that consumers responded to most.

We also tested the advertising. It outperformed all the historical advertising on Crisco, including work I had been part of years before featuring the country singer Loretta Lynn. Best of all, the advertising appealed to younger consumers, and the recipes were a critical element as these consumers were still gaining meal-planning experience.

We now had great advertising and a strategic media plan. We had also expanded the campaign to include more recipes and a focus on holiday cookies. I knew the advertising would drive sales and revenue for Crisco. But we had a limited budget and planned to start the advertising in late October. I wanted to jump-start the effort and begin in September. I gave the advertising and media agency the go-ahead to do this.

Starting the advertising a few weeks early may not sound like a big difference, but it was. Essentially, I was forward spending the budget. If the advertising didn't work, I would be reducing the profitability of the brand. I did not have the authority to do that.

The other complication was that I was promoted just as the advertising was due to launch.

This turned into a major issue. Because the advertising started earlier than planned and at the end of a fiscal quarter, the profitability for Crisco and for the sector housing the brand was below target. Even though I took full responsibility for the decision directing the agency to run the advertising earlier than planned, P&G threatened to fire the advertising agency. I wrote a memo stating unequivocally that I owned the decision and had taken it to grow the business.

In the end, Crisco had a holiday quarter that outperformed all expectations. Even with the added expenditure of advertising, the brand delivered profit levels that had not been seen in years. I stayed on that business for another year as the associate advertising manager and delivered strong results. But I had killed my career because of the unauthorized spending. I was a dead man walking. It was time to get out.

I look back on that experience and recognize that while I had the right idea, I executed poorly. My gut instinct to invest in the advertising and marketing for Crisco to drive revenue and profit was correct. Also, once a business has momentum, it creates a great overall environment. People want to work on these businesses. Creativity is unleashed, and new ideas are implemented.

But I had overstepped my authority. I should have written a great one-page memo to convince my management to invest in the advertising. I should have lobbied for support and generated excitement for the proposal. I should have been transparent and invited others to be part of my thinking.

I would apply these lessons at my next role.

THE SO WHAT

Mistakes happen. We never learn without making mistakes. When you make a mistake, own up to it. Too often, we make excuses or blame others. The critical first step in learning is to own the mistake yourself.

Then, believe it was a mistake. Be honest: it didn't work! You made a bad decision, and the results don't lie.

Learn from it and endeavor to never make that same mistake again.

5

ALMOST KILLING A BRAND

One company that had repeatedly tried to hire me away from P&G was PepsiCo.

During my time within P&G's soft-drink business, I had significant exposure to both Coca-Cola and PepsiCo. They were the dominant players. Each had a significant bottler network responsible for making soft drinks from the concentrate sold to them by the parent organizations. Crush, Hires, and Sun Drop were bottled and sold into retail by a mix of Coca-Cola and Pepsi distributors. Our brands were an "add-on" that provided revenue opportunity for the distributor and flavor variety for the consumer. Distributor relationships were geographically defined, so Hires could be with a Coke distributor in one market and a Pepsi distributor in the immediately adjacent market. This made the launch of national campaigns challenging, as I had to negotiate with both local distributors and the national Coke/Pepsi organizations to gain support. It also gave me significant exposure to the senior leadership of both organizations.

PepsiCo had tried to get me to join their Frito-Lay organization in the mid-1980s. Neither the timing nor the brand (Rold Gold pretzels) were right. But after my fiasco with Crisco, I was more open to alternatives.

DISRUPTING THE PIZZA BUSINESS

The right opportunity within the PepsiCo organization was to become the divisional marketing director for Pizza Hut in 1991. PepsiCo owned three restaurant companies at the time: Kentucky Fried Chicken, Taco Bell, and Pizza Hut.

In the western division of Pizza Hut, I would be geographically responsible for almost one-third of the country, from Oklahoma north to the Dakotas and west of Texas. I had four peers representing the balance of the US. Our jobs were to create and implement regional marketing initiatives to augment the national programs produced by the Wichita, Kansas headquarters.

My region was growing the fastest as we were adding new delivery and carryout locations. Historically, Pizza Hut had dominated the branded pizza category with dine-in locations. Because land was expensive in the highly populated markets in my region, the number of "red roof" dine-in locations was limited. But the delivery and carryout locations—"delcos" for short—had a much smaller footprint and were more economical to build. The western region was leading the country in transitioning from red roofs to delcos.

At the time, red roofs and delcos differentiated not only regions but also the company-owned restaurants from the franchisee-owned ones. Franchisees tended to be in the smaller markets where the red roof restaurant still attracted families for a night out. Franchisees often preferred to add delivery capability to this restaurant, versus building a separate delco.

Marketing programs were decided by committee. There was a National Co-operative Association with representation from corporate and from franchisees. Each group had two permanent voting members. The deciding fifth vote was determined based on which organization—corporate or franchisee—was generating the majority of revenue. The fifth vote had swung to corporate just before my arrival.

Local co-ops worked in a similar fashion funding local media and marketing initiatives. Votes were tallied based on revenue. I held the voting majority at the local level up and down the West Coast—except in Spokane, Washington.

At the national level, plans were made for a dine-in push behind Personal Pan Pizzas and the 11:00 a.m. to 2:00 p.m. lunch part of the day. I was new to Pizza Hut, but I knew this was a disaster for my western region. We had more than a thousand dedicated delcos; these locations didn't even serve the Personal Pan Pizza! Even in our traditional red roof locations, lunch was a very small part of the overall revenue, and you couldn't grow it enough to drive the overall performance of the restaurant.

National-level agreement to this program had been a "gimme" to appease the franchisees. Historically, these efforts had become less and less effective. But corporate had declined to use its deciding fifth vote to overrule the proposal.

My idea was to layer a delivery/carryout advertising message on top of the national Personal Pan Pizza effort. This way we could push sales throughout the day and have a powerful message for our delcos. But I got a ton of flak from national marketing at corporate. They felt I was not a team player because I was not supporting the national message with additional local co-op marketing funds. The only support I received was from the national media-buying director. He was a key ally as I learned the restaurant business, and he had a very good understanding of my region.

I shared with him the idea of using a West Coast media feed to efficiently support the delivery/carryout message. Television advertisers could buy a West Coast media feed to deliver commercials across all markets up and down the coast more efficiently than buying spot media in every market. The media director knew the efficiency of this approach and had been trying to execute this for years, but there was one problem: I needed the support of all the affected local co-ops, and I didn't have the votes in Spokane to push this through by myself. I needed to get this local co-op on board.

LEARNING TO ENROLL OTHERS

So, I journeyed to Spokane to speak with the local co-op chair and to convince him that this was the right call for his business and the business of other franchisees in the market. It was hard work and entailed many visits and phone calls. In the end, I convinced him based on pure data.

Lunch revenue for the typical red roof restaurant was less than 15 percent of the total; delivery and carryout were more than 60 percent. Without marketing support, revenue for delivery and carryout would be lost to competitors or to missed impulse purchases. I used a variety of revenue simulations to show him that even for Spokane-area red roof restaurants, there just wasn't enough upside in the lunch part of the day and the nationally supported marketing push to offset stagnating sales for their main revenue segments. Even in franchisee restaurants, they needed to push delivery and carryout to grow revenue and profitability.

I had learned from my Crisco fiasco. While I knew I was right, I required allies. I needed to go through the formal process, getting each co-op to approve my plan.

THE SO WHAT

Enrolling others to support your ideas is a critical skill—one that isn't taught in business school. No matter your role, you typically are always trying to "sell" a new idea or new way of approaching a problem. To do this effectively, you need to understand the perspective of others facing the same problem. What do they believe is the best solution? What problems do they see with your proposed plan? How do you marry these two thoughts to get to the optimum solution?

Addressing the objections of others is the first step to enrolling them into your idea. You need to show how your approach can solve their issues and concerns.

Once others are convinced, have them advocate for your idea. Forging alliances really is the only way to move a disruptive idea forward.

The West Coast media feed happened to be supporting a Hawaiian-style pizza with ham and pineapple. We used the *Hawaii Five-0* theme song, and the spot was brilliant. The West Coast restaurants had strong delivery and carryout results. Nationally, including our restaurants with dine-in, the lunch business grew dramatically with the Personal Pan Pizza program. But it wasn't enough, as I had predicted, to drive growth overall for the chain. Only the western division generated overall revenue growth during this time frame, and it was all because of the West Coast feed and balanced approach. This was a big, early win.

PRECURSOR TO A PROFESSIONAL SWITCH

During this time, I was learning on another front—one much more personal. While I had played video games at the home of friends and at the video arcades of my youth, I finally bought my own gaming console. It was the Super Nintendo Entertainment System, the SNES.

The system came packed in with a game: *Super Mario World.* I would play this game endlessly. I was transfixed by the music, the game play, the ability to swim and fly as Mario. In the end, I finished the game and all its hidden locations with ninety-nine lives—the maximum you can have. It was a testament to skill but also to using information from magazines like *Nintendo Power* and *Electronic Gaming Monthly* to beat the levels and collect lives. I became a dedicated gamer. It reflected my "completionist" mentality: I needed to finish 100 percent of a game. This fueled my competitive spirit and my desire to win—whether it was a video game, a marketing campaign, or anything else I did.

Every weekend I would venture out to the toy and hobby stores selling video games to find something new to play. I owned and played more than seventy games for the system. Much later, when I would be the executive vice president of sales and marketing for Nintendo of America, I would learn that the average owner of the system had about eight games. I was a super user of the Super NES.

I didn't think a game would capture more of my attention than *Super Mario World,* until I started to play *The Legend of Zelda: A Link to the Past.* The game became a second job for me. I would spend the day creating and implementing marketing programs for Pizza Hut and then come home and play *Zelda* after eating dinner and continue deep into the night. Playing this game demanded both strategy and ingenuity. Strategy because I had to make choices regarding how I would approach a particular part of the game, choosing between brute force to beat the enemies or choosing to pull back to gain more health. Ingenuity because I had to solve the game's puzzles to progress.

I was so challenged by the game that when I couldn't figure out one puzzle on my own, I called the Nintendo Game Play Hotline for help. The first time I called, they gave me general suggestions to solve the puzzle. When that didn't help, I called back. "Look, I just called a little earlier and the other counselor gave me only general suggestions. I need the answer!" After a few seconds, he did give me the answer. Later, as a Nintendo executive, I learned that doing so was taboo. But I was certainly grateful.

My son and eldest of my three kids also became hooked on the game. He had his own game file. Before bedtime, he would watch me play. When he would get home from school, he would look to see how far I had progressed without him and play up to that point on his own game file.

After progressing through the game one evening, I was at the final boss battle. Beating this enemy would complete the game. At this point, it was around 3:00 a.m., and I would have to be up in a few hours to ready myself for work. I stopped to get a couple hours of sleep, but during my working day all I could think about was getting back to the game.

I walked into the house that evening to the sound of my son squealing with excitement. My heart sank. I knew exactly what had happened. He had found my file and had spent the next few hours trying to beat the final boss. He had accomplished this just before I had walked in the door. He was able to watch the credits for the game, which I would never get to see as this played only the first time a game was completed. Later, when I was at Nintendo, I would tell this story in front of more than a thousand gaming industry executives when Mr. Shigeru Miyamoto, the creator of the franchise and producer of that game, was recognized as an industry champion by the Entertainment Software Association. Mr. Miyamoto even asked me, "Reggie-san, is that story true?" And I assured him, "Yes, Mr. Miyamoto, it is true. This is how you touched me and my family even before I became a Nintendo employee."

ADMITTING WRONG, GOING RIGHT . . . FAST

In the spring of 1993, I would get a call from the head of marketing at Pizza Hut asking—demanding—that I relocate to Wichita to head up a critical project. My division had been selected to test-market a new product called Bigfoot Pizza, but now he wanted me to manage the project from the corporate headquarters as part of the national marketing team.

The US was experiencing a recession at the time. One competitor, Little Caesars, was flourishing by selling two carryout pizzas for one low price. It didn't matter that the flavor or texture didn't compare favorably to Pizza Hut. It was a lot of food for a low price, and that was what families wanted. Bigfoot Pizza was our answer. It was one rectangular pizza, two feet long by one foot wide. Bigfoot Pizza sold at the same price as Little Caesars, but we also offered delivery in addition to carryout.

I managed the test market and the overall initiative. Bigfoot Pizza drove huge revenue and profit growth for the company. We had to figure out how to manage the capacity of the restaurant as each pizza took about ten minutes to bake. During the dinner rush, the output was nonstop. As part of managing the testing, I spent many evenings in Pizza Hut restaurants going through the dinner rush and being exhausted from trying to keep up with demand for Bigfoot Pizza.

It was my job to convince the National Co-operative Association to launch Bigfoot Pizza nationally. I ran into the same issue as my West Coast advertising feed initiative—delivery and carryout were not as important to franchisees given their red roof traditional restaurants. I had to open additional test markets, this time including franchisee locations so they could experience the positive growth for themselves. Even though they did see significant revenue growth and were also threatened by Little Caesars, they were tough to convince.

In the end, they supported the initiative, and Bigfoot Pizza won an innovation award when it launched nationally.

I was responsible for monitoring the business results for Bigfoot Pizza. About six months after launch, market research was showing a troubling issue. To sell the massive Bigfoot Pizza at a low price, the product was made with a different crust and different cheese than the traditional Pizza Hut product. In fact, they were inferior to the traditional Pizza Hut pizza as quality came with a cost. The market research began to show that consumers were noticing the difference.

Bigfoot Pizza's thinner crust would frequently burn at the edges if the sauce and cheese were not properly applied. The cheese, because of its higher fat content, would wick oil and make the overall pizza a little soggy if not fully cooked. We were willing to accept these negative product reviews for Bigfoot Pizza, as these issues were similar to Little Caesars. But consumers were beginning to rate the regular Pizza Hut pizza negatively, even though these recipes had not changed. This was unacceptable.

I took these results to Pizza Hut leadership and now advocated that we make plans to exit the Bigfoot Pizza business. Imagine this turn of events: the same person who had worked so hard and argued effectively to launch Bigfoot Pizza was now arguing to wind it down.

I made my point. I showed how our product perception scores were falling and we were at risk of losing this core benefit of the brand. I also showed how we had weakened Little Caesars and needed to shift our attention to other competitors—Papa John's for example—that were pushing a product quality message. It was the right thing to do for the long-term health of the brand, and eventually Bigfoot Pizza came off the national menu. It was foundational learning for me. I had launched a product that generated almost a billion dollars of revenue, had won awards doing so, and then had to shut down that same business. The experience reinforced the need to think long term about initiatives, and to push for the right decision no matter how painful. I also recognized the value of acknowledging a mistake and quickly pivoting to a better solution.

THE SO WHAT

Long-term thinking is a difficult skill to learn. Often we want the immediate gratification from a new idea or initiative. Leaders learn to think downstream and game-plan the full range of results from a particular decision. Don't be frozen in this thinking and delay making a decision. Form a hypothesis: if we do this, then here is what may happen. Positive outcomes are great; but how do you mitigate the negative outcomes? As your web of hypothetical options becomes more successful, move forward with confidence.

6

BEING TOO POSITIVE

I was fortunate that early in my career I learned which facets of running a business excited me. I love pace. A business that is constantly evolving is exciting to me. This is why I enjoyed the restaurant business so much and why later I would thrive in the worlds of entertainment and video games.

I also love complexity. I love thinking deeply about a business, its issues, the potential solutions, and then game-planning those solutions to understand the downstream implications. I saw others who were stuck and frustrated dealing with complex issues. For me, it was an invitation to dig in, solve problems, excite consumers, and drive the business forward.

I learned to step back to see the big picture, think critically about the challenges, and to be strategic to overcome them. And I learned when it was appropriate to pivot to small issues that had big consequences if they were not addressed early. Being able to balance this thinking—telescoping to see the big picture in one meeting to drive strategic attention and then microscoping into the details for the next issue—became a core competency for me.

THE SO WHAT

I have found that managers are effective in either understanding the big picture or managing details. But the best business leaders can do both and are comfortable shifting from one skill to the other at the appropriate time, maybe in the same meeting.

INNOVATING A WORLD-CLASS BUSINESS

At Panda Management Company (PMC), the parent organization for Panda Express and Panda Inn, I put these behaviors into practice. I went to PMC from Pizza Hut. This was my first role as a department head and my first time to sit on an executive leadership team for an entire business.

PMC was a privately held and family-run business that was transforming itself into a high-growth company by building new restaurants and progressing toward an initial public offering. Unlike other categories in the restaurant industry, there was no market-leading chain for Chinese food. Instead, this category was—and still is—largely made up of individual mom-and-pop restaurants. As a consumer, you were never sure what you were getting when you visited your local Chinese food place. High quality and consistency of the food are critical. A friendly staff eager to answer questions about specials is also a differentiator. Panda Express sought to be the gold standard across all these factors in becoming the first nationally branded Chinese food chain.

The very first Panda restaurant was a full-service Panda Inn started by Andrew Cherng and his father, Master Chef Ming-Tsai Cherng, in 1973 in Pasadena, California. Andrew's wife, Peggy, was also instrumental in growing the company from these restaurants to the fast-casual version: Panda Express.

In 1994, the Cherngs hired an accomplished restaurant industry executive, Joseph Micatrotto, with the goal of creating a world-class restaurant company. I was recruited the following year to lead the marketing organization.

The role was everything I wanted at the time. While the marketing organization was small, I brought disciplined thinking and a focus on food innovation to it.

At the time, Panda Express was largely a food-court restaurant. The Panda iconography stood out in this setting. The food was exceptionally high quality, and during the midafternoon lull at the mall, Panda Express staff would be in the common area right outside the food court offering samples to potential consumers.

I pushed to execute more of this type of inside-out marketing, leveraging the traffic of the mall to increase visits to our locations. I also elevated the tactic of creating new dishes and thematically promoting these flavors alongside Panda's bestselling dish: Orange Chicken. Orange Chicken would typically be selected by more than 60 percent of guests when they would order a two-item combination platter. But Orange Chicken was very costly to make as it was a multistep process to prepare the chicken, flash-fry it in a batter, then wok-fry it again with the spicy orange sauce.

Working with Panda's head chef, we created a vast range of dishes that looked and tasted great and cost less to make than Orange Chicken. This was a win for the consumer and a win for the company. We created promotional themes for these new recipes that increased our foot traffic even more.

AN ASPARAGUS PROBLEM?

We were at the start of one of these themed promotions, "The Taste of China," featuring one of my favorite dishes: chicken and asparagus in black bean sauce. Consumers were loving this dish too; it was being chosen on about one-quarter of all meals. But I received an urgent visit by our head of procurement, David Parsley. David had been hired about the same time as I, as part of the team to lead the company to an IPO.

"Reggie, we have a problem," David said. "There is some sort of blight with asparagus. The cost to us is doubling over the next couple of weeks, and it could go even higher than that."

This was a huge issue. Asparagus was already one of our more expensive vegetables we were using during the promotion. David had been a key partner in garnering organizational support for the recipe and its inclusion in the promotion. With costs increasing this dramatically, we would face pressure to either pull the dish or to pull the promotion altogether.

We convened a team to work through options. In addition to asparagus, black bean sauce had been a special item we had introduced into Panda Express just for this promotion. We needed to be thoughtful so that this item would not end up as a wasted cost.

We pivoted to a chicken-and-broccoli dish with black bean sauce as a new feature to be included in the promotion. Broccoli was already a staple ingredient in the restaurants—buying more would not be an issue. And this recipe would use the balance of black bean sauce we had already procured. We rushed to have new food photography done and to reprint the promotional materials. It would take two weeks to change over to the new recipe and supporting marketing materials. David managed the transition on the raw ingredients side, making sure we had enough asparagus in the short term and then purchasing incremental broccoli to support the promotion.

It was a classic example of stepping back to understand the breadth of the problem and its potential impact on the financial health of the company, and then getting into the details to solve the problem in an effective way.

Solving difficult business problems often has cascading benefits beyond the immediate solution. In this situation, there were two.

David and I were already close, but this experience solidified our professional and personal friendship. The experience also gave me credibility throughout the organization, especially with our restaurant operations team. These relationships were invaluable with the next challenge I faced.

THE STREET STORE CONCEPT

For PMC to execute a credible IPO, we needed a strong growth story. Sure, the company was expanding by adding new mall locations and by increasing the individual store revenue in most locations. But management recognized that only a finite number of high-quality mall locations existed—even in the mid-1990s. To capture investor enthusiasm, we needed to have a restaurant that could be placed on any street corner in the world—a "street store" that would compete with a local mom-and-pop Chinese restaurant but could also innovate with delivery or drive in.

Panda had already tried to execute this concept but had failed. Essentially, they had taken the mall store and placed it outside. The food presentation was still in a steam table visible to the consumer. There was little external marketing. The menu was the same as what you would find in the mall, with a focus on combination plates versus family-size servings more suitable to be eaten at home. It was no surprise that these locations were not working.

I was charged with creating the next-generation street store that would fuel the IPO.

My selection was not universally supported. My doubters asked: What does this marketer know about operations or store-level economics? What about real estate knowledge? Finding the right locations for these new Panda Express restaurants would be critical.

While I certainly had been exposed to all these issues during my time at Pizza Hut, it was also true that I was no expert. Often leaders will be given a challenge in which they don't have all the skills or background at the start of the project. There are two key ingredients for success in these situations: a compelling vision and the capacity to learn quickly from outside experts or experience. In this situation, I had a vision for what the Panda Express street store concept should be. And I had the ability to ask questions and learn from the internal experts to bring my vision to life.

My vision was for a Panda Express restaurant that served all the great-tasting food the chain was known for. Plus, expanding the menu to enable consumers to visit the restaurant frequently and never tire of the choices available. We would offer limited seating and combination platters for guests who wanted a dine-in experience for lunch. The main focus would be on takeout, with planning for delivery and drive-thru in the future.

The restaurant operations would need to change. No more visible steam table; most of the food would be cooked to order. We needed more wok cooking stations, but different sizes as some items would be cooked in larger batches based on that location's experience with prior guest ordering. More wok stations also meant a larger area for washing and keeping a flow of clean woks. We would need to better manage the guest queuing so that there would not be congestion by the cashier stations.

We also needed to up our marketing game. Initially, we would start with high-impact local marketing that I had learned during my divisional marketing job with Pizza Hut. These were local direct-to-consumer mailers announcing the opening of the restaurant and showcasing the menu. We also needed to plan for success and think about how many locations would be needed to scale the marketing, incorporating mass-market communication such as radio or television advertising into the mix.

The vision I painted was very different from options the company had considered before. I forced the exploration of a wide variety of ideas. My task force team visited a range of fast and casual restaurants in search of innovation—including restaurants outside of the Chinese or Asian food categories. We took many ideas from these other concepts. "Steal and reapply" would become another mantra for me.

These new Panda Express restaurants looked and operated completely differently. This meant I had to learn from every expert within the company. I asked questions of our operations leaders to learn about all the tasks that most consumers never see in a restaurant. I spent time in our Panda Inn locations to take some of their food preparation processes and adapt them for our new concept. As we created new procedures, the operations team needed to be convinced they would work. New ideas always face resistance. But these experts were included in the process to define the steps, test them, and optimize the results. This is the only way I have found to overcome initial resistance.

I accompanied our real estate experts to hand-select the locations for our first two test stores. We wanted to have one location that was zoned for drive-thru as this would be part of our experimentation. The other location would be more neighborhood focused, with some businesses nearby that could support the restaurant's lunch rush. Balancing lunch versus dinner volume had been a key learning from my Pizza Hut days.

The new street store concept would need different cashiering versus our mall locations. These would need to link to a food prep ticketing system so that the chefs would know what they needed to prepare.

In the end, I needed to sell the entire concept to the executive team and the board of PMC. Most importantly, I would need to sell this to Andrew and Peggy Cherng. They were the most important and most challenging. They were the experts, having built this business with their own hands. They saw the complexity of the concept I was proposing. But they also were aware of the detailed plans for executing this new street store, and they saw its potential.

The first of the new stores was built in Manhattan Beach, California. I visited the store as it was being built. When the kitchen was finished, I was there for initial food-prep testing to make sure the flow would work as we imagined. We simulated a peak hour of orders to pressure-test the operations. We found flaws that needed to be fixed. It was stressful and invigorating as we approached launch day.

THE SO WHAT

Successful innovation always starts at the core: the main equity of the existing company or brand, or the key problem that you are trying to solve.

Become insightful about your business and the key levers of profitability. Be perceptive about what your brand means to consumers. In particular, how it is differentiated from other offerings the consumer can choose.

For Panda Express, the great-tasting food and the great overall experience powered by the employees were at its core. We changed just about everything else in the new street stores. But the food, and the experience, differentiated the restaurant from competitors and delivered on the brand's core benefits.

ALL THE RIGHT MOVES, NOT ALL THE RIGHT OUTCOMES

Overall, the economics of the street store concept demanded an average unit volume of one million dollars a year. This was an extremely high bar to clear given that it required more than three times the volume compared with the actual performance of past company street stores.

The Manhattan Beach location opened at a significantly higher revenue than our target and grew from there. Consumer feedback was universally positive. Food quality was exceptional. And even though we were serving many more consumers than we had initially forecasted, guest wait times were manageable. The store was a huge win for the company and for me personally.

The second location, in Studio City, California, did not fare so well. We were delayed in permitting as we worked to get the store footprint right in order to enable drive-thru. Entering and leaving the drive-thru would take up more of the land than we were initially told. We fought with the city for months, delaying construction. This location never did open during my tenure with PMC.

My time with Panda was cut short as Andrew and Peggy changed their mind on executing an IPO. Even though we now had a street store concept that was proving itself to be the growth engine for the company, they decided they wanted to grow more slowly as a privately held company.

One by one, the executives that had been brought in left the company. We had come from larger organizations betting that we could take this great company to a dramatically new level. Being part of a well-run but small operation was just not what we had signed up for.

My conversations with Andrew and Peggy were especially heart wrenching. They loved the work I had done and painted a picture for me that had me potentially running the company. I loved them as people and told them so. They had put their trust in me with the new concept store, and I had grown through that experience. But as founders and majority shareholders, they would always make the final decision. And just like the decision to change course and not execute an IPO, they didn't always follow the facts. At that point, I made my decision to leave the company.

THE SO WHAT

There are situations in which you have done all the right things to achieve success, but staying the course is no longer viable. This applies both in a business and a personal context. Be clearheaded in these situations and understand the reality of what you face. At that point, make the best decision, without resentment and without blame.

THE ALTERNATIVE PATH

All my family was on the East Coast, and I focused my job search there. I had one opportunity in the restaurant industry and another back in my consumer packaged-goods roots. In my now tradition of pursuing the alternative path, I chose to leave the restaurant industry.

The alternative path was with Guinness Import Company, the sales, marketing, and distribution company handling Guinness stout and a collection of other premium imported alcoholic beverages including Bass ale, Harp lager, and Pilsner Urquell and Red Stripe pale lagers. In addition to the great collection of brands, a key deciding factor was my boss-to-be, a fellow ex-P&Ger named Gary Matthews.

Gary and I didn't work together at P&G. He left P&G to work at PepsiCo, and we didn't run into each other there, either. But we shared a common framework for business strategy and brand building. And we shared a passion for moving fast and for aggressive revenue growth.

Working with Gary at Guinness reaffirmed a couple of key points for me.

First, you don't always need brand-new ideas to drive strong growth. Executing the hell out of existing ideas can also be fantastic. When I joined Guinness, the brand had already been executing a promotion offering consumers a chance to "Win Your Own Pub" in Ireland. The concept of winning a pub and enjoying a lifestyle of pulling Guinness pints and living in Ireland was a dream come true for brand aficionados. The team that had created the idea was already leveraging the promotion in bars and in public relations. But the promotion had not yet been aggressively pushed in retail stores.

Guinness was just launching a draught product in a can with a widget that would release nitrogen into the stout when the can was opened. Nitrogen creates the cascading effect and thick head when a pint of Guinness is poured. Nitrogen also delivers the smooth, creamy mouth feel of Guinness, versus the bite you get from a typical lager containing carbon dioxide gas.

I challenged the organization to use the "Win Your Own Pub" promotion to drive retail activity in conjunction with Guinness can draught. It was a huge success. Consumers loved the product and the innovation of the widget. Retailers loved the program because of the higher margins and profit that imported beers deliver versus domestic brands.

Capitalizing on existing but underutilized ideas with superior execution is a great way to make your mark. The company had an entertainment concept called the Guinness Fleadh. A *fleadh* is a music and lifestyle festival based on old Irish customs of dancing and music making. Just as I was joining Guinness, the team executed the first Guinness Fleadh in New York City. It was a two-day event, and the main business driver was that only Guinness Import Company brands were served during the event. For the local distributor, this was a success, but the event had no impact on the business beyond the city.

I worked with the team to take the Fleadh to three cities the following year—New York City, Chicago, and San Jose—and to use the broader geographic coverage to generate retail activity across the US. At retail, Guinness stout, Bass ale, and Harp lager were all featured. This generated significant volume lifts for all the brands. The program was a hit, and we worked to put in place a growth plan for the Guinness Fleadh that would continue to add cities every year.

THE NATURE OF BOSSES

Second, my time at Guinness taught me a lesson that may seem obvious but is one that rising managers fail to grasp: you cannot succeed without a great boss.

As a result of the strong business results we generated at Guinness Import Company, Gary was promoted to run a significantly larger business for Guinness in the United Kingdom. Because I was still relatively new at the company, I didn't get his job—instead, it went to an executive from Guinness's Ireland branch.

Maybe it was the challenge of being an expat and having to learn the complexities of US liquor laws; maybe it was the pressure of continuing the high-growth performance of the company; maybe he just wasn't up to the task. Regardless, my new boss decided I was the reason why he wasn't succeeding in the role. In an early performance review, he said, "Reggie, you are just too positive . . . too optimistic."

"Tell me more."

"You are always looking to make ideas better. To make people better. Sometimes you just need to cut and run."

Needless to say, I did not stay at Guinness much longer after that conversation. The guy was toxic, and I wasn't learning or having fun.

Luckily for me, my prior boss, Gary, wasn't enjoying the Guinness UK experience either. He left to lead a private equity–backed venture in the bicycle business called Derby Cycle Corporation, where the company would buy strong bicycle brands with the goal of cobbling together a powerful global network. He asked me to join the venture as chief marketing officer.

THE SO WHAT

Great bosses add value. They build on your ideas. They help you navigate office politics or difficult peer relationships. They leverage their own experience to teach you and to help you grow. The best bosses are not threatened when their subordinates are actually better than they are; in those situations, a great boss will both learn from you and get out of your way.

Sometimes you will have just an average boss. In these situations, as long as you continue to learn and contribute, you can do well. But when you have a boss who is toxic, get away as fast as you can. If you love the company, push for an assignment away from the bad boss. If you can't do this, look elsewhere. Toxic bosses leave a trail of good people running away from them. Eventually, this catches up to them, and they move on to run a different team, division, or organization into the ground.

A NEW BUSINESS CYCLE

The global bicycle industry at the time was highly fragmented. There were only a handful of big brands, with the biggest being the component company Shimano. Because of this structure, bicycle company margins were low.

Derby sought to compete differently. We had the Raleigh, Univega, and Diamondback global brands. We also had a number of strong regional brands, such as Gazelle in the Netherlands and Focus in Germany.

As part of my role, I had responsibility for product development. This meant bringing product managers from all the countries together to discuss best-in-class features for the different bicycles we offered. I wanted to harmonize the specifications for all our different types of bicycles. I believed that a great road bike should be similar in France or Italy or the US. The same would be true for mountain bikes or kids' bikes. But at the time, each product manager had a slightly different specification. The business was already complex because we offered all different types of bicycles—kids', mountain, road bikes, and so on. Without a harmonized product development process, we were buying hundreds of thousands of different component parts.

By coordinating our approach, we would use our size to gain negotiating leverage with component companies like Shimano. And with best-in-class designs, we would be able to have better quality bicycles and improve our margins at the same time.

We would also apply leading principles of marketing and sales to a very sleepy industry. We created world-class television advertising for Raleigh and Diamondback. We trained our sales team to work with the independent bike shop owners to better merchandise their stores.

And we envisioned an internet strategy in which you would be able to order a bicycle online from an extensive catalog of brands, specifications, and colors and go to your local bike shop in a few days to pick it up, get it fitted to you and tuned up, then bring it home. It was a big idea because local bike shop owners have limited space and limited credit, so on-hand inventory can be thin. We could literally offer hundreds of bicycle options to the consumer.

We were already shipping bikes to our current distribution network of retailers, so there was no incremental cost to us in this approach. As we learned about consumer preferences, we would manage our inventory at the warehouse level, giving us significant advantages over even the largest store operators. While we would capture more margin in the initial bike sale, the retailer in our network was not overly threatened as they would create a direct relationship with the consumer we drove into their store for the final fitting of the bike. At that point they could sell helmets, clothing, and other accessory items that have a very high margin. And they would service the bikes at the end of the season, or the beginning of the next one. This was a disruptive idea back in 1999.

Overall, the strategy was working. We created great bicycles and the consumer responded positively. We tested the internet bike shop idea and it worked. We created a business plan for the private equity partners that showed how the business would grow dramatically.

The private equity partners were spooked, however. The bicycle business uses a tremendous amount of cash during its business cycle. Parts need to be ordered in the fall, and the bikes are built in the winter. Then they are shipped to the bike shop owners in the spring. These are small-business owners requiring credit, typically sixty days. Cash would not be flowing to Derby Cycle corporate until summer . . . nine months after the heavy expenditures on the component parts. Even with credit from the component manufacturers, the cash conversion cycle was very long. Our private equity investors needed to provide the additional cash to fund the growth plan.

Private equity doesn't like this business model. They prefer businesses that don't require a lot of cash. We scared them by showing our business growth plans and the amount of new cash we wanted them to invest into the business. They demanded that we scale back our plans and go for slower growth. We were being too positive.

The management team wasn't supportive of this slow growth plan, so once again I was part of a high-flying team that disbanded.

This is another important lesson. There are times you believe you have found the perfect new job or the perfect new role within your current company. You fully invest yourself into connecting with your colleagues, learning the details of your new opportunity, and creating a great work plan. But things can still go wrong.

Sometimes the role is wrong for you, and you don't have the required skills. In this case it is your responsibility to ask for help and get the training you need. There is no shame in this, and most managers will jump right in to give you the required help. The best managers will teach you and show you what needs to be done—but they won't do it for you. They want to make sure you learn the required new skills from the training experience.

Other times, the organization's leadership isn't buying into your plan. In this situation, you need to truly listen to their objections and understand the critical points they are raising. Then you need to communicate additional information to try to overcome their objections. This means new information or new data, not just a re-presentation of old facts and old perspectives.

On rare occasions you will have gathered all the new information and believe even more passionately in your proposed plan. But management is still not buying it. At this point you have two very clear alternatives. Accept defeat, align with your organization, and move forward to the next initiative. Do this in a positive way, believing that your organization just has more insight and perspective at this point. And do this with your complete self, without bad-mouthing management.

Or move on and transition to something else—again, without remorse and without bitterness.

What you cannot do is to stay in the current role or organization and subvert the decision that you didn't agree with. This behavior is disruptive to the entire organization and creates a lack of trust that is devastating.

THE SO WHAT

No matter the situation, choose your next steps. Sometimes you will find yourself in a situation in which you feel strongly that you're right, but the powers-that-be tell you that you're wrong. Be thoughtful, analyze your situation, and game-plan your alternatives. Are you just reacting to your wounded ego? Or do you believe you're right but in the wrong position in the wrong company with the wrong leadership?

You always have alternatives.

7

BEHIND THE MUSIC

This was a very challenging time for me. Personally, I was going through a contentious divorce and making sure my three children understood that the breakup of the marriage had nothing to do with them. My sons were fifteen and eleven at the time, and my daughter was five. Each child had difficulty with the divorce, and I spent a lot of time with them to work through the situation.

Professionally, I was also in a difficult place. Between Panda, Guinness, and Derby Cycle, I had changed roles every two years. While each change provided increased responsibility and global experience, the "jumpy" career path did not look good on paper. I needed to be extremely thoughtful about my next role.

I leveraged my network to take meetings with a range of executives and search firms. Since my days with P&G, I had created valuable connections across industries, and it was in this moment that these were most helpful. Despite my concern that my résumé showed a series of short two-year stints, I was generating strong interest from blue-chip companies in the New York metropolitan area where I lived at the time.

In particular, I was having highly positive meetings with executives from PepsiCo. Steve Reinemund was the CEO, and we had overlapped briefly at Pizza Hut. Steve wanted me to take a role within the Pepsi organization. It was a big job, with great people working on the business. I saw myself doing well there. But to a certain extent, it would have been more or less what I had done and disliked at P&G: grow a business modestly and generate some efficiencies to create profit growth.

The other opportunity was something completely different. I was interviewing for a role within Viacom's entertainment business to be the senior vice president of marketing for VH1, part of MTV Networks.

PERSONAL INTEREST AND NEW CHALLENGE

This role excited me on multiple levels. My boss would be John Sykes, an MTV pioneer. John was there when the idea for a music-video channel was born and had led the early marketing department. During the interview process, John and I had great conversations. He loved the work I had done at Derby Cycle to create relationships across all the different business units and develop cohesive strategies to move the business forward. John shared that VH1 was going through a challenging period of figuring out what was next for the channel beyond their big hit *Behind the Music* and the special events they produced such as *Divas* and the *VH1 Fashion Awards*. Everyone had a different point of view. He needed someone to help coalesce a vision and then drive it forward.

The role at VH1 also dovetailed with my love of music. As a boy in Brentwood, I had shared a bedroom with my older brother. There was always music playing in our bedroom; when we were young boys it was initially Motown, then Elvis Presley. My brother introduced me to the Rolling Stones, Jimi Hendrix, Janis Joplin, and Bob Dylan. Together we listened to Led Zeppelin and Cream. I started to drift to more pop: Fleetwood Mac, Stevie Wonder, Elton John, and Billy Joel.

Our bedroom had all the posters from these albums on the wall, plus each of us had one large poster by our beds. His was Jimi Hendrix, caught in the middle of a guitar solo, eyes closed, with a bandana across his forehead. Mine wasn't a music poster; instead it was Steve McQueen from the movie *The Great Escape*. He is on a stolen motorcycle, with the prison in the background. The visual spoke to my drive to "get away" and pursue big dreams. I also appreciated McQueen's roles in which he was typically doing things his way, disrupting the status quo. He always found a way to get things done.

With the influences of my brother's tastes and my own love of music, I had a massive collection of records and tapes. I made mixtapes for my drives from Long Island to Cornell. I badgered the DJs at our fraternity parties to play the best music to keep our parties going and the dance floor full. To this day, I still love to discover new music.

While VH1 was looking to transition into its next incarnation, music was still at the heart of the channel. Music videos were still being played—albeit in the overnight hours and early mornings. Artists were still having impromptu acoustic performances in our lobby and at MTV.

Most importantly, the entertainment business was a new experience for me. When faced with the choice of doing the same as before or doing something different, my bias is always to choose something different. I believe this fundamental desire pushes me to innovate and disrupt. Because I want to try new and different experiences, I unpack why they are appealing to me. This forces me to put new ideas in context and to consider how to make them relevant to the consumer while satisfying a need in unexpected ways. "Relevant, but unexpected" is another mantra for me. I used this thinking to create award-winning advertising for products as diverse as soft drinks and shortening.

VH1 was the first time I was in a content business driven by creative talent. Consumers choose to spend time watching a show because it is compelling to them. Producers and writers are the critical talent who craft the shows to hook the consumer. Executives like me read scripts and review early versions of a show to make changes in the margins. If the raw creative talent doesn't exist or cannot be unleashed, the content just won't be great.

This was a huge change for me. In all my past roles, I was a key driver of the product. I would shape the strategy. I would drive the agenda. Not this time. I had to adjust my approach to be more collaborative and suggestive.

ENTERTAINMENT COLLIDING WITH THE INTERNET

I spent time with the show producers to understand how they were thinking about the content and how to bring the content to life. Additionally, I worked with the creative team who generated the messaging that appeared in between the programming. These creative packages—called interstitials—could be the difference between a viewer staying tuned into VH1 after a program ends or changing the channel to watch something else. I grew an appreciation for how important this messaging was. In my future role at Nintendo, I would focus on how we messaged to our consumers, leading them from one game or event to the next and making sure we always had their attention. We would create our own marketing content for the new age and take the idea of interstitial communication to a higher level.

In addition to valuing creative talent and learning how to work with creators, my VH1 tenure helped me deepen my understanding of the internet and envision how gaming, entertainment, and the internet would come together. An initial key partner in this journey was my friend Jason Hirshhorn. Jason is a typical New Yorker, a brash fast-talker and a fellow lover of music. He had started an internet company in the music space that was purchased by MTV Networks in 2000. Jason was learning the culture within MTV just as I was coming into the company. We hit it off and spent considerable time talking about VH1's nascent website.

At the time, VH1's website was just a deeper catalogue of its show listings. Information on the programming was there, and you could see titles for shows coming up later in the day. Even by the standards of 2001, the site was not very strong. The site wasn't "sticky"— consumers had no reason to stay on the site for any extended period of time. Jason was pushing for more music-oriented content, streaming videos, or having a music player, for example, to keep visitors engaged.

I was pushing an additional agenda: how to better monetize the site. We sold sponsorships to the programming on the VH1 TV channel, and banner ads were provided on the website essentially at no incremental value. It was a vicious circle: the website didn't keep visitors engaged so overall traffic was low; low traffic meant a low value to advertisers; without added revenue, it was difficult to invest in upgrading the website. The site remained a poor experience, and we needed to break this circle.

My idea was to create new content to drive visits and engagement. While Jason pursued music, I pursued games as the vehicle.

As an entertainment executive, and as a player, I knew gaming was on the march to dominate more and more of a typical consumer's time. This was especially true for the target audience of VH1: adults twenty-five to thirty-four. I wanted to create gaming experiences that would live on VH1's website and would tie back to the programming and extend consumer reach and engagement. We would sell sponsorships against this content as a revenue driver for the channel.

There was an added benefit to this idea. Because no one at VH1 had any gaming-related experience, I could drive the idea myself. I tapped my resources to find quality developers who would be interested in creating content that would live on the VH1 website. During that process, I was fortunate to find Guha and Karthik Bala from a small studio in upstate New York called Vicarious Visions.

THE SO WHAT

Successful innovation is part of an organization's culture. No matter your role, look for ways to add value to your organization beyond your current responsibilities. Great ideas truly can come from anywhere and from anyone. Encourage this behavior as part of your leadership role.

This doesn't mean that you pursue every new idea. But keep a running list; test the ones that seem strong and require little incremental resources. For the bigger, more complicated ideas, have a process for evaluating the ideas with an eye toward balancing revenue potential and cost to execute.

The Balas and I hit it off immediately. They had been developing games since high school, and they had recently won awards at a big gaming developers' conference. Their games had the right balance of challenge and fun to keep players engaged. The Balas realized that while they were creating games on a longer timetable for platforms like Nintendo's Game Boy, they also needed to execute smaller projects that would create cash flow for their small studio. They fit my criteria for a quality development organization open to new ideas and new revenue streams. The Balas and I would continue to work together during my Nintendo years.

The gaming project was gathering momentum until September 11, 2001.

A LESSON IN CRISIS MANAGEMENT

While most New York City executives in the media and entertainment world start their day between 9:00 and 10:00 a.m., I was an early riser to navigate my commute from Connecticut. I would typically be at VH1's Times Square office around 8:00 a.m., earlier if I had morning meetings.

On that fateful Tuesday morning, I did have a morning meeting, so I was in the office by 7:30 a.m. I had two televisions in my office, the usual setup for media executives. The TVs were typically muted. One was always set to VH1 so I could see the programming at any time. I would rotate the other television to news, sports, and other programming depending on the time of day. That morning, I had the second TV set to *The Today Show*.

Members of my team were gathering in my office for a 9:00 a.m. meeting as *The Today Show* was showing visuals of fire and smoke coming from the North Tower at the World Trade Center complex. At that point, speculation was that it was an accident involving a small commuter plane, so we continued with our meeting. My back was to the TVs as one of my employees gasped and pointed over my shoulder. This was when the South Tower was hit. We turned up the volume and listened to the broadcast. Within moments, it was clear that the plane had purposefully hit the second tower. I told my team to head back to their offices and to prepare to go home.

My assistant Connie had commuted into the office from Queens and was also an early arriver. I asked her to contact all my external appointments and cancel for the day. I watched *The Today Show*'s broadcast for another few minutes as speculation continued to build from believing this was an accident to speculating that this was a terrorist attack.

My thoughts were spinning when Connie, her face now ashen, called to me from the doorway of my office. "Reggie, building security is on the phone. They need to talk with you."

Security never called an executive. There are specific individuals responsible for building operations at each channel and in each business unit. If there is some sort of issue, they are the ones contacted. This is why Connie was so shaken.

I got on the phone and was told that building security had been working down a list for each business unit to get to the most senior executive who was physically in the office. I was the one for VH1.

"Mr. Fils-Aimé, we believe there may be more attacks. Ours is one of the tallest buildings in Midtown Manhattan, and we may be next. We are evacuating the building, and we need you to work with us to clear out the VH1 floors."

This shook me out of my stupor. For the next ninety minutes, I went from office to office telling staff members what was going on and that they needed to leave. I was only six months on the job, and for some of the staff in larger departments, I was talking with them for only the second or third time. I had to balance compassion with firmness depending on the situation. Some staff needed no encouragement to leave. Others who were working on a deadline needed a firmer push. For some, I had to circle back a few times to make sure they had packed up and left the building. I performed a final tour with building security around 11:00 a.m., and after sending Connie home, I confirmed the VH1 floors were secure. At this point, both towers had collapsed. I grabbed my bag and prepared to be away from the office for a few days. No one was truly sure what was going on. All we knew was that our building was being closed, and it was unclear when it would reopen.

My next challenge was getting home to Connecticut. Under normal conditions, my door-to-door commute was about seventy-five minutes using the Metro North train out of Grand Central Station. I got to Grand Central, and it was bedlam. There was a heavy police presence, and the main concourse was filled with anxious commuters like me trying to get home. The public announcements stated that train service was suspended and there was no indication it would resume. I was stuck in New York City.

I knew the area surrounding Grand Central like the back of my hand and headed next door to the Grand Hyatt Hotel. There is an interior walkway connecting the two, and at the time there was an area with monitors showing the departure times and track numbers for trains leaving Grand Central. There were also TVs showing a variety of programming, all now tuned into news channels. Here, I could monitor the situation and figure out how to get back home.

I was fortunate that in this area of the hotel I was still able to get cell phone coverage. I had connected with the owner of the car service I had used for years. He said he had other clients like me who were stranded in Manhattan and needed to get to their homes in Connecticut. He asked if I would mind sharing a car with a few other executives and potentially having to make a few stops as others were dropped at home before me. "Not a problem," I said. "I will be happy just to get home!" The only downside was that I would have to wait up to three hours before getting picked up, and the drive would also be extended because traffic was a mess.

As soon as I hung up, I saw a message on the screen that rail service would resume shortly. I hustled back to Grand Central Station in time to hear that train service was about to begin but that all trains would be stopping at every station to get commuters home. This would probably add an hour to the train ride, but I would get out and be home before the car service alternative would have even picked me up.

I was fortunate to get on one of the first trains leaving the station, and after getting a seat and canceling the car service, I finally had a chance to close my eyes and reflect on the day. I realized that I was lucky. I was far away from the devastation, and I was getting to go home. I opened my eyes to see a man in my train car, sitting alone covered head-to-toe in white dust. Clearly, he had been much closer. In this crisis, I had focused on the tasks at hand, gotten them done with a clear head, and kept moving forward. No panic. No drama. Just got it done and moved on.

THE SO WHAT

Regrettably, traumatic events seem to be happening with an increased frequency. Leaders are acting as "consolers-in-chief" to help organizations work through these difficult times. Authenticity, compassion, and consistency with values are critical. I believe it is wrong to ignore these moments. But be principled in how you approach them. A tone-deaf response will harm your and the company's reputation.

The balance of the week was a blur. The office building remained closed for a few days, but work still needed to be done. In the fall of 2001, the media business wasn't healthy because the economy was still in decline from the dot-com bubble's bursting the previous year. Many of the early tech companies were heavy advertisers, which had been a positive force for media companies at the turn of the century. As these companies went bankrupt later in 2000, they took their advertising dollars with them, leaving big revenue holes for media companies. As a result, VH1, along with all the sister companies that were part of Viacom, was planning to execute layoffs in the fall.

We also had the day-to-day business of the channel to manage. VH1 had a marquee event planned for October 19—the *VH1 Fashion Awards*. This event was a major revenue generator as it attracted advertising from cosmetics and fashion companies that otherwise did not spend much on the channel.

September 11 also galvanized the media and entertainment industry to help those affected by the terrorist attacks. The first event was broadcast just ten days later and was called *America: A Tribute to Heroes*. It was a worthy event, with major musical artists performing and celebrities working phone banks to take pledges of monetary support. But the event had no live audience for the performances, and so it felt dark and somber.

MAKING MUSIC: TUNING IN TO UNIQUE SITUATIONS

My boss, John Sykes, had a different vision. He imagined a more uplifting event held in New York City as both a tribute to the spirit of the city as well as a fundraising effort for first responders directly affected by the tragedy. So, along with the regular work of VH1, we set off to create a coalition to produce what would become The Concert for New York City.

The workday evolved to one where regular work for VH1 was conducted until about 7:00 p.m., and then work would shift to planning for the concert. We had team meetings every evening until about 9:00 or 10:00 p.m. Once or twice a week, we would have executive meetings with John and his peers from Madison Square Garden/Cablevision, Miramax, AOL-Time Warner, Sony Music, and more. This was a massive undertaking. There were direct and tough conversations about every detail including the lineup of performers, presenters, and producers of the short films shown during the event. Egos were bruised and then needed to be repaired. We pulled together an event in weeks that normally would have taken six months of planning.

As the marketing lead, I had no budget. Everything I did was based on the value of trade (you do this for me, and I can do this for you) and the power of relationships. I was still new to the media industry, so I was often meeting executives and asking for favors in the same meeting. I had to assess how I could also help them achieve their objectives while still getting what I needed.

I also was pulled into issues where I had no knowledge or expertise. For example, I had to coordinate with international media outlets that would run the concert in their markets but were prohibited locally from raising funds for charity. For these markets, I had to coordinate a unique satellite stream of the show that did not have the scrolling information for how to donate. I addressed the issue by asking questions and then came up with immediate solutions.

The Concert for New York City happened on October 20, 2001. It was more than four hours long and generated more than $35 million in relief for those directly affected by the September 11 terrorist attack.

The day before, VH1 taped the 2001 *Fashion Awards*.

Major back-to-back events planned during the same time and produced within the same twenty-four-hour span was unheard of. This causes you to focus on what is important and problem solve with urgency. You learn how to shift from big-picture strategy to the minute detail of execution. You lean into established relationships to ask for help and support. And you create new, lasting relationships.

During this time, the relationship with my now wife, Stacey Sanner, was born.

By the time I arrived at VH1, Stacey had already been with the channel for more than five years. She was a director in public relations reporting to the senior vice president for PR, my peer. Stacey had years of experience in the music industry working for Restless Records in Los Angeles and A&M Records in New York. She was also the key liaison on the publicity side of The Concert for New York City. She and I were in all the planning meetings together, and a few weeks before the actual concert, I invited her to dinner. I framed it as a discussion for me to learn about the channel and how to navigate the culture of MTV Networks. We had a great time at a small Italian restaurant a few blocks away from the office. We talked about everything but work. It was far more than dinner; it was the beginning of the rest of our lives together. I didn't know it at the time, but she would be one of the casualties of the massive layoffs that happened just a few weeks later. This allowed our relationship to continue without the glare of an office romance, and she would have a series of great roles within the media and entertainment business herself after VH1. She would eventually follow me out to Seattle.

8

NINTENDO COMES CALLING

Despite my wins at VH1, I was having difficulty not being in control of the direction of the channel. I always wanted to be driving the agenda for the business I was involved in. Even in my junior roles at P&G and Pizza Hut, I was always leading key tranformational projects that would shape the future of the business.

I was not doing that at VH1. This was the role of the key executive in charge of production at the channel. While I certainly provided my perspective on the content, my role was more in support of the shows that were produced. Essentially, I was responsible for driving consumers to watch the first few minutes of our programming. It was the role of the creators and producers to keep the viewers watching with compelling content.

The recession and market turbulence put my gaming initiative for VH1 on indefinite hold. Advertisers were still tightly controlling their budgets and did not yet see the value of digital marketing. Plus, the layoffs within MTV Networks made the pursuit of new initiatives that were not tied to revenue nonstarters.

As an added issue, my MTV mentor, John Sykes, was promoted from the channel to be chairman and CEO of Infinity Broadcasting, overseeing 185 radio stations reaching more than seventy million weekly listeners. This was a huge role for John, and I wished him well. But I knew I would also miss his mentorship.

By the spring of 2003, I was ready for a change. I began discussions across a range of companies and industries, looking for a role where I could apply all my skills and abilities.

I received a call in the late summer that year from a recruiter on behalf of Nintendo. They were looking for their next head of sales and marketing.

A LEADER NO MORE

Nintendo was in a difficult situation. Two years prior, for the 2001 holiday season, Microsoft had entered the video game business with its Xbox platform. Nintendo had launched its home console, GameCube, at the same time. But both systems were being dwarfed by Sony's PlayStation 2 that had launched the prior year. Game systems are driven by the software available on the platform. The large game developers and publishers are motivated to support platforms that have a large consumer base and with whom they can negotiate financial support.

Sony had a number of advantages with its PlayStation 2. First, they had succeeded with their prior system, the original PlayStation, and chose to enable games made for that legacy platform to be playable on the PlayStation 2. This backwards compatibility was a first for home consoles in the gaming industry, and it assured that it would be easy for PlayStation owners to upgrade to the new system.

Second, Sony was using disc-based technology as the medium for its games. Replication costs were very low for discs, compared to Nintendo's cartridges in their Nintendo Entertainment System (NES), Super Nintendo Entertainment System (SNES), and N64 platforms. This gave PlayStation an economic advantage, as their games generated more profitability for developers. This instilled tremendous loyalty on the part of developers, often resulting in the best independent publisher to put their games on the Sony platform either first, or exclusively.

Third, Sony was introducing DVD technology into the overall consumer electronics space, and its PlayStation could be used as a stand-alone DVD player. In fact, PlayStation 2 cost the same or lower than basic DVD players. This opened up gaming capability to any consumer looking to have a home theater.

Nintendo's GameCube and Microsoft's Xbox sales were each less than one-third of Sony's PlayStation 2 sales by the time I received the first recruiter call for the role of executive vice president of sales and marketing for Nintendo of America Inc. I had witnessed the decline of Nintendo in my own household as I still had my Super NES and my N64 systems connected to my television. But a new system had shown up alongside—a PlayStation 2. Just before I had taken the recruiter's call, an Xbox had entered my living room as well. I had all the current gaming systems—except for Nintendo's GameCube.

I was a regular customer at the local GameStop, Best Buy, and Toys "R" Us stores and would routinely talk with the retail associates at all three. They spoke enthusiastically about PlayStation 2. Many were also excited about the connected capabilities of the Xbox, even though they had a much smaller lineup of exclusive games.

When I would ask about GameCube, they would suggest that units were increasing in their back inventory, meaning that units were not selling in stores and product was clogging up the supply chain.

While Nintendo was having challenges with GameCube, they were dominating the handheld market with Game Boy. In 2001, they had introduced an upgraded model, Game Boy Advance. Nintendo had used backwards compatibility on this platform to their advantage. GBA, as it was nicknamed, was a runaway hit. Nintendo leveraged all their intellectual properties such as *Mario* and *Legend of Zelda* to drive their handheld business, and late in the original Game Boy life cycle, they had introduced the phenomenon *Pokémon*.

Sony had always looked at Nintendo's handheld dominance with envy. They had dominated portable electronics with the Walkman music player in the 1980s and 1990s. They wanted to do the same in the gaming market. So, at the 2003 Electronic Entertainment Expo, commonly called E3, Sony announced their intention to enter the handheld gaming market with the PlayStation Portable. All they did was announce the name, and Nintendo's stock price declined more than 10 percent with the news. Nintendo was about to be attacked on its most profitable business, and the only business that had maintained an iron grip on market share. This was the backdrop to my conversations with Nintendo about their potential role for me.

OPPORTUNITY OR DEAD END? MAKING A CRITICAL CAREER CHOICE

I talked about the opportunity with all my trusted mentors and associates. Just about all of them counseled me not to pursue the job.

"They are in decline."

"Working for a Japanese company is high risk."

"In the Pacific Northwest, you would be away from your family and friends."

"Gaming is a small business with a poor public perception."

All their statements had an element of truth. But I saw something different.

I knew the industry as a consumer. I had been playing video games on and off since junior high school. I knew firsthand how Coleco and Atari had captured attention, then failed with a glut of bad games. I had watched Nintendo breathe new life into the gaming business with a focus on innovation and the highest quality games. And I saw in my own home how Nintendo was now losing ground to Sony and to Microsoft in the current generation.

I also knew Nintendo's franchises. I had played all the *Mario*, *Pokémon*, and *Smash Bros.* games. And I loved the *Zelda* franchise. I saw how my love for the games was shared with my children and how they expanded their own gaming experience. This suggested to me that the gaming industry would grow significantly as their age group had income of their own. I also imagined a future where they would share their own love of gaming with their kids. I saw an industry with a bright future—if it was well managed.

THE SO WHAT

Tough career choices are coming at young professionals with greater speed and urgency than in the past. Navigating these decisions requires critical thinking and "gut" instinct.

Do your research. In addition to reading all the publicly available information, investigate the company. Try out their services; talk to their customers. Score their strengths and weaknesses. Do they have the capabilities to win long term? Do your skills match what is needed?

But you also need to apply your instinct and experience to the problem. This includes your own experience as a consumer of the product or service, as well as experience with competitors.

Also, think about the culture. Can you fit in?

And once you decide to go forward, you need to be all in and follow through to the very best of your ability.

I created pages of notes on key issues facing Nintendo and how I would solve them. Despite advice from friends and mentors to the contrary, I decided I could make a difference for Nintendo and went all in.

The process started with a series of videoconferences with the recruiter. I would learn later that these were recorded and shared internally with Nintendo of America (NOA) staff. Based on this material, I was asked to visit the NOA headquarters in Redmond, Washington. I spent a long day meeting with former and current executives including Peter Main (the very first sales and marketing EVP for NOA), Howard Lincoln (former chair of NOA who left to be CEO of the Seattle Mariners baseball club, which was majority-owned by Hiroshi Yamauchi and Nintendo of America at the time), and Tatsumi Kimishima (at the time, president of NOA).

My visit was almost scuttled when I had a very active conversation over lunch with Flip Morse, the head of human resources at NOA. I asked Flip a few basic questions about employee development and training. "Reggie, we don't do much of that here. We are a subsidiary of a Japanese company. They don't believe in the 'people' stuff."

"Wow, Flip," I started. "I have a completely different view. I believe developing the organization and investing in people are fundamental. Without a strong organization that is learning new skills, it is very difficult to meet new challenges."

This back-and-forth went on for some time. It raised significant concerns for me. At this point in my career, I knew that the only way an organization could be successful was to have strong people at every level—a strong leader at the top was never enough. I also knew that you needed to spend time with staff to train, develop, and coach them for superior performance. Every leader needed to make this personal investment.

My concerns were eased in a follow-up conversation with Howard Lincoln. "Reggie, of course strong leaders at NOA invest time and energy with their staff. I did it all the time. The fact is the EVP of sales and marketing is one of the most important jobs at NOA.

You will have tremendous latitude. And what you do will be noticed by the entire organization. If you show how to invest in the development of your team, it will catch on and be replicated throughout the company."

ASKING FOR WHAT YOU NEED

My appointment to the role was jeopardized a second time. During my research and recruiting process, I recognized I would need strong working relationships with the executives at the Nintendo Co., Ltd. (NCL) headquarters in Kyoto. And the most important relationship would need to be with Satoru Iwata, who had been appointed global president in May 2002. I asked to have a videoconference with him.

I found out years later that this had caused major issues at NCL and NOA. "Who does he think he is? This request is unheard of! Our global president has more important things to do than to meet with Reggie!" In retrospect, and now with my full understanding of the Nintendo culture, I can see how my request would be perceived as unconventional. Maybe even arrogant.

To lead the sales and marketing function effectively, though, I needed to know the direction of the company and to have confidence in its leadership. Selfishly, I also needed to make sure that I would be successful at Nintendo. It was a high-risk role. The company was being challenged.

My videoconference with Mr. Iwata was set for thirty minutes. It lasted much longer than that. I had anticipated there would be a translator in the room, but he was alone. This made the meeting much more intimate, as he controlled the cameras to zoom in and make it appear as if he were just across a table from me. He asked what he should call me. "Please, Mr. Iwata, just call me Reggie."

"Mr. Iwata, how do you view the systems by Sony and Microsoft?"

"Reggie, while we try to understand the other companies, Nintendo believes in taking its own approach. We create new experiences. We create games that are unique." We talked in detail about the past innovations Nintendo had brought to the market such as the directional pad, 3D visuals, rumble feedback in a controller, and four-person multiplayer. I had experienced all of this on my Nintendo systems at home.

"I have been visiting retailers. They tell me they have a lot of GameCube inventory and that something must be done to spark sales right now."

"Reggie," he said, "we have plans to spur sales in the next few weeks. We understand that it is important to generate momentum now, in the early fall, versus just waiting for the holiday season." He shared that they were preparing to announce a price decline to spur sales, and they were already hard at work on a successor to GameCube.

Lastly, I asked him about PlayStation's entry into handheld gaming. "Mr. Iwata, how will Nintendo compete and address this threat to the company?"

"Reggie," he said, "accept the job and come to Kyoto. I will show you how we will continue to innovate."

After this intimate video conversation, I was sold. I was confident I could work with Mr. Iwata and support his visionary leadership. And I knew I could apply my skills to help transform NOA to a world-class organization.

THE SO WHAT

It sounds counterintuitive, but the perfect time to ask tough questions is when you are being recruited for a role. The company likes you—you would not have made it to the latter stages of a recruitment process if they didn't. At this point, make sure the company and role are right for you. Ask penetrating questions. Assess the answers you receive. Look for consistency in the answers from senior leaders—this tells you if management is on the same page. Be respectful . . . but push.

9

KYOTO CRAFTSMANSHIP

As I joined Nintendo, I was committed to applying my twenty-plus years of experience across a range of industries and business situations to the challenges at hand.

I immediately scheduled business reviews across all elements of the sales and marketing division. My purpose was twofold: to learn about the business from the experts on my new team, and to engage and connect with the people. I asked the department heads to bring every member of the team to the business review. We went around the table making introductions, and I was always the last person to make introductory comments. I was driving home a message that I put them first and that I wanted to learn from every team member.

A GAMER AND A BOSS

This led to some funny moments. When performing the business review with the team running *Nintendo Power* magazine, I asked the leader a question. "In 1993, I sent in a photo of my son after he had beaten the *Super Street Fighter* game on the Super NES. He was only three years old at the time. Why didn't *Nintendo Power* publish the photo? Or even send us a letter to celebrate this achievement?"

This was a true story. The game was a bit of a button-masher, meaning as long as you kept pressing buttons your character would fight and make some progress against the opponent. If you lost the fight, you would simply fight that character again and not lose any ground. As long as you eventually beat your opponent, you would progress to the next fighter. So beating this portion of the game was inevitable, as long as you kept pushing buttons. Still, I was the proud father of a three-year-old video game champion, and couldn't resist touting the accomplishment.

I raised this with the *Nintendo Power* team to demonstrate that I had a history with Nintendo's content as a player. I also wanted to communicate that I wasn't a furious tyrant. I've been told that when I concentrate, my brow furrows and my eyes become fixed into a stare. A slight frown often slips onto my face. In other words, I look like I want to tear you apart.

In the team meeting with *Nintendo Power*, my attempt to humanize the boss by telling the story about my son didn't work. I was the new and unknown big boss and had asked a direct question.

The department head stammered for a moment and then said, "Reggie, I don't know why we didn't publish his photo. Let me go back into our archives to understand what happened and who made the decision."

"No, no, no," I said, "don't do that. I am just having fun here. We are in the entertainment business, and I was just trying to lighten up the room. Just know that I have a legacy with our content. And that I have a sense of humor." Word spread that the new boss knew the games and was a good guy. Mission finally accomplished.

THE SO WHAT

Be approachable and "human" as a boss. Your team needs to know that you have their, and the company's, best interests at heart. They need to feel your support. In return, you require *their* support. Be confident that the team will break through barriers and do whatever is necessary to execute initiatives with excellence in order to support you.

Being best friends with your employees isn't necessary; leading with empathy and heart, as well as with vision, are the requirements.

ESTABLISHING RELATIONSHIPS, BREAKING SILOS

In my early days, I made a point to connect with all my peers as well. I met with each one: leaders for finance and IT, business affairs, licensing, operations, and product development. Operations and product development were critical focus areas for me as we needed to implement a series of new sales initiatives to recapture momentum, and I would have to partner with these functions to create the plans.

THE SO WHAT

Whether you are a newly hired university graduate in your first corporate role or the veteran expert hired to shake up an organization, discover and understand the complex web of relationships and activities unique to the situation. Who needs to be your key partner? Where are projects getting stuck? Where are the opportunities for fresh ideas and new approaches? Apply your immediate attention to these areas. Invest time in these relationships and ask open-ended questions. Gather information, then make your plan and begin engaging these key constituents.

Operations was led by Don James. Don was a very early employee at Nintendo of America, either the third or fourth person hired into the company depending on whom you asked. At this point, he had already worked for the company for more than twenty years and had deep relationships with Nintendo developers in Kyoto. Don had witnessed Nintendo's transition from an arcade game developer/manufacturer to console game developer/manufacturer. Don knew all the historical successes and failures of global Nintendo. And given his tenure, he had spent time across many of the company's disciplines, including game development, game testing, manufacturing, and logistics. When I joined, he was responsible for managing NOA's total supply chain, from the time product left Asia to the moment it arrived at retailer loading docks.

Don also had another very special role within Nintendo. He was the guru of Electronic Entertainment Expo (E3)—the most important trade show in the world for gaming. He had played a key part in the transition of video games being a minor part of the Consumer Electronics Show (CES) to then creating its own trade show. Don worked with the developers in Japan to understand the new game systems and game content to be shown at this annual event, and to solve the complex technical problems for showing off these innovations to more than fifty thousand attendees of E3.

Given Don's role as head of operations and de facto head of E3 planning, I knew he needed to be a key partner. Luckily, we hit it off immediately. We shared a passion for scuba diving and for straight talk. But I would learn quickly that we had a key difference. I am a "glass half full" type always looking for opportunity. Don was the opposite, a "glass half empty" guy who saw downfall in every situation. When we would be discussing new ideas or E3 plans, his favorite words were always, "We're doomed." It took me a little while to realize that this was just his code for "Yeah, that might be tough but I will get it done."

Product development was led by Manabu "Mike" Fukuda. Mike was technically an employee of NCL as he was a Japanese national. But he had been working in the US for more than twenty-five years, including time at a number of companies before Nintendo. Mike was a senior vice president, ostensibly junior to me in my role as EVP. But it was critically important that Mike and I work effectively together. He spoke directly with the executives and game developers at NCL. He was privy to inside information that I needed to know—game development schedules, potential for development delays, and overall quality of the content. I required an unvarnished perspective from Mike, and the only way to obtain it was to be trusted with this sensitive information.

I was entering this relationship with a deficit. Unfortunately, members of sales and marketing had not treated information with confidentiality in the past, so he was reluctant to share. Mike also did not like the direction of the advertising and the advertising development process. I would need to win Mike over.

I took a multipronged approach with Mike reflecting the need to connect with him emotionally and rationally. First, I set up biweekly meetings with him to understand Nintendo's historical approach and its business culture. But these meetings would transition to discussions about our future product plans overall. I made the important decision that these meetings be held in his office, not mine. I wanted him to know that I saw him as a peer, even though his title was junior to mine. And I wanted the entire organization to see me heading to his office, versus the other way around. This symbolic gesture carried weight in the NOA culture.

CLEAR PROCESSES THAT YIELD GREAT RESULTS

Next, I created transparent processes to solve historical pain points between his organization and mine, with a focus on the advertising development process. Advertising development is a pain point in most organizations. There are both strategic and technical steps that lead to great advertising. And there is an art to it as well, a feeling you get when you hear a fantastic slogan or visualize a key insight for the very first time. Everyone always has an opinion on new advertising. Great campaigns have many parents; a bad campaign is an orphan no one claims responsibility for.

Having faced this issue before, I created a step-by-step process map for how we would create advertising at Nintendo. I knew from my earliest days at P&G that compelling advertising would be necessary for reinvigorating growth. At each step in advertising development, there needed to be clarity on who was responsible for recommending the action, who owned the approval of a decision, who would be consulted at that step, and who would need to be informed on any approvals. Creating this RACI model (Recommend/Approve/Consult/Inform) was contentious. This may sound very boring, but this discipline is key to effective marketing.

Marketers and advertising agencies want to own every step in the development of marketing ideas and consult no one along the way. This often leads to advertising that is either off strategy or painfully ineffective. Other departments, like product development, seek to be consulted at every step. This creates a time-consuming process that invites opinion from individuals who are neither trained nor experienced in advertising development.

I made sure Mike and members of his team played key roles in our advertising development. For example, they were responsible for approving the product brief so that the marketers and the advertising agency fully understood the product and what made the game or system compelling.

There were steps I needed to own fully. Approval of the advertising strategy. Approval of the final proposed concept. Approval of the final finished commercial. Each of these key steps requires clarity and decisiveness—approval by committee never works here. One person needs to drive this, and own the result. I made it clear that I was that person in the EVP role.

Initially, this did not sit well. Not with members of my own team who felt that they, as director for advertising or SVP for marketing, needed to own these steps. Nor did it sit well with Mike or members of his product development team. Even my peer EVPs felt they needed to play a role in this decision.

No. I made it clear that the only way to get truly world-class advertising was to have a transparent and collaborative process, but at the end only one person owned the key strategy, development, and final execution decisions.

THE SO WHAT

Driving profitable revenue growth is the ultimate objective for a company leader. Delivering a differentiated benefit to your customer is the key to achieving this.

Delivering: communicate what it is that your product does. Whether it is a physical product, a service, or an emotional benefit, describe it in a compelling fashion and then actually perform that benefit. Vaporware doesn't survive in the long term.

Differentiated: stand out from your competition. Ideally, in a positive way!

Customer: understand your customer better than anyone else. This way you can uncover unmet needs and focus your product development efforts.

Using this process, we created world-class advertising for Nintendo beginning with Game Boy Advance SP in 2004 and continuing until I retired in 2019 with Nintendo Switch. As president, I relinquished all approval rights except one. I maintained the decision whether any advertising developed by NOA would run. This assured that I played an active role in the advertising development process and enabled me to have the ultimate decision to keep bad advertising from being aired.

Lastly, with Mike, I invited him into the sales planning process. This is where we would create specific initiatives for our key retailers. The Nintendo approach was to have a base menu of programs for all retailers and then additional programs that were unique to the retailer and funded by a formula based on their sales revenue of Nintendo products. This made the approach fair and equitable across our retailers but rewarded retailers who grew their business with us.

Historically, this was managed within the sales organization without much oversight. I had a fundamentally different approach. I wanted to invite discussion on these programs to make sure we were pursuing big and bold ideas that would have a more dramatic impact on the business. And I wanted to get away from purely price-related programs as I felt this negatively affected the equity value of our brands and franchises.

My approach started with participation by marketing executives. Before me, the marketers had little influence on sales initiatives even though both functions reported to the same divisional boss.

Next, I invited participation from Mike. Partly this was to educate him on the sales challenges we faced. But I also wanted to get his ideas on new products and new approaches, and to enlist his support for any radical ideas that would need approval from NCL. As appropriate, we would need to get Don involved for any initiatives that required supply chain support.

Using this approach, we created a program where retailers were given an opportunity to promote unique items to their consumers—their own unique color Game Boy Advance or unique bundle of GameCube hardware and game, as examples. These programs were short-term wins for the organization and for the business. Organizationally, we were breaking down communcation barriers within the company and reinforcing a culture of teamwork. The business was being stablized with these programs as they performed well in the marketplace. I was building credibility as a leader beyond just sales and marketing.

THE SO WHAT

Strong leaders balance individual decision-making with collaboration, but there are certain decisions that only the leader should make. Even so, collaboration and consensus building are important steps. Leaders are constantly evaluating this balance as organizations shift. With newer staff in place, for example, a leader may need to make more of the decisions. More experienced teams function best with higher levels of discussion and collaboration.

LEARNING TO SPEAK NINTENDO'S LANGUAGE

It was during this time that I made my first trip to Kyoto and the NCL headquarters. This was January 2004, and I was just eight weeks into my time at NOA. I was in Kyoto for a week, having individual meetings with key NCL executives and attending a series of global leadership meetings. It was during this time that I first met Mr. Iwata face-to-face. We spent a couple of hours together during the week continuing our discussions about the current business and about the future of Nintendo.

During the first couple of days, we also conducted early planning for my first E3. Don arranged a series of meetings with key creators to review games and to discuss their progress in preparing materials for the trade show happening in May, just four months later. One of these meetings was to review a special prototype of Nintendo's next handheld system. At this point the system didn't have an agreed-upon consumer name.

I walked into the room and saw the prototype laid out on a large, flat motherboard with exposed chips and soldering. At the center were the defining two screens of the system. As I learned the touch and voice activation capabilities, I felt as if I were plugged into the motherboard—the electric shock of unlimited potential shot through me. The excitement in the room was palpable, and the hair on the back of my neck stood. The prototype was fully functional and the developers showed us a variety of different games. This was the Nintendo DS, a system that would go on to sell more than 150 million units globally during its life span.

Don and I were the lone non-Japanese in the room. Information was shared in alternating translation, from Japanese to English. Any comments we made in English would then be translated into Japanese. This made for long meetings, and it was a process that I would get used to over time. We were discussing the system's touch-screen at length and how this would enable new forms of game play. Touchscreens were not yet a mainstay in consumer electronics, as this was well before the iPhone. Only personal digital assistants utilized touchscreens at the time, and these were high-priced products and not mainstream.

As the new senior executive responsible for sales and market-ing in the largest subsidiary at Nintendo, I was expected to make comments even though I was new to the business. I jumped right in. "The touchscreen is a major differentiation for us," I began, even as I peripherally saw a staff member open the door to let a new-comer into our closed-door meeting. "We will need to feature this in our consumer communication. What games make best use of the touchscreens?" The team went on to describe a new experience in the *Metroid* series and a new *Mario* game. But the developers were most excited about a game they were developing where you use the touchscreen and the built-in microphone to interact with a virtual dog. "We need to fully leverage the touchscreen. We need to make this a key message at E3 and paint a vision for the new experiences that Nintendo developers will be able to create," I said.

Once this was translated into Japanese, the man who had arrived stepped more fully into the circle that had formed around the Nintendo DS prototype. It was Shigeru Miyamoto, the creator of legendary franchises *Mario*, *Donkey Kong*, *Zelda*, and so many others. He had been the late arriver and had been present for my questions and comments about the touchscreen. My knees began to shake a little.

"He is right," said Mr. Miyamoto in Japanese. "The touchscreen needs to be a major focus for us. And we need to work hard on the experiences we plan to showcase at E3 and demonstrate how we will create brand-new games for consumers using all the capabilities of our new system."

After this was translated, he continued. "By the way, who are you?"

This was my introduction to Mr. Miyamoto.

It was also the beginning of my indoctrination into the concept of Kyoto craftsmanship. Internally, this described the precision and detail of everything within Nintendo. The craftsmanship of the developers is plain to see as Nintendo games dominate any list of top-rated games in history. But this also reflects the attention to detail in every aspect of Nintendo's business.

Nintendo's spiritual connection to craft can be traced back to before the Meiji period, when Kyoto was the imperial capital of Japan. Even when the capital moved to Tokyo around 1868, the emperor and senior lords of Japan would travel back to Kyoto for fine linen, glassware, sake, and other goods. The uniqueness, unparalleled quality, and pride of the Kyoto creators is renowned.

Nintendo's founder, Fusajiro Yamauchi, created *hanafuda* ("flower card") decks to circumvent a ban on gambling. Because of their beauty, those cards remain popular to this day and are still sold.

Now the world also sees that excellence every day in Nintendo's games.

10

KICKING ASS AND TAKING NAMES

Now that I had seen the prototype for the Nintendo DS and some of the early game concepts, it was time to focus on preparations for E3.

I invested time to watch the presentations from 2002 and 2003. I dissected the messaging and the presenters. I looked back at the press clippings and the fan engagement. There was a lot of opportunity for improvement.

E3 was a massive event, the coming together of the entire video game industry for most of a week. Physical presentations would have more than a thousand skeptical journalists in the audience. But the presentation would be streamed to a worldwide audience of millions of eager fans.

Company and personal reputations were at risk. Judgments would affect a company's stock price or retail support for new products. E3 presentations needed to be perfect—but when I reviewed the previous two years, I saw that the performance was lacking.

My biggest observation was the lack of a unifying message. What do you want the audience to walk away with? What is the big idea? How do the games and the key facts support the message?

TELLING THE RIGHT STORY

I view big presentations as a narrative. I want to take the audience with me on a journey. So, you start with a bang and end with a bigger bang. Not every part of a presentation will be a hit, and often a presenter knows in advance when the audience is likely to get uninterested. Great presentations counter these lulls with a change of pace to get the audience back on your side and eager for more.

After viewing past presentations, I asked those involved why they had made particular decisions. Why did the 2003 presentation begin with a dry review of facts and figures versus showing off what the audience wanted—new games? Why had a version of *Pac-Man*—a twenty-three-year-old game at this point—been shown? In 2002, some presenters were holding on to their notes onstage . . . not the most inspiring approach to convince the audience that they knew their stuff.

During this process, I connected with a key partner, Don Varyu— not only for my first E3 but also for my entire time at Nintendo. Don was a senior executive at our PR agency, Golin Harris—later just known as Golin. He started his career in news journalism, which was a key asset in identifying story angles and crafting messaging to bring these stories to life.

By the time I met Don, he had already been supporting Nintendo for more than ten years. He knew the industry and the inner workings of Nintendo as well as anybody within the company. From the early days of the NES to the console wars with Sega and then PlayStation, Don had been there. Most importantly, just like me, he was eager for Nintendo to make a comeback.

Don and I began to meet regularly, and he began interviewing me like the reporter he used to be. The goal was to get to know me, understand my motivations, and most importantly to learn my voice. Instead of starting with my early memories, he focused on the here and now.

"Reggie, why did you come to Nintendo? Why are you here?"

I explained my history with the company as a player and my knowledge of all of Nintendo's franchises, including *The Legend of Zelda*, my favorite. I wasn't just a hired gun to try to help turn the company around; I had a passion for the industry and for Nintendo.

We talked at length about my competitive streak. How I focused on "winning" by driving positive change wherever I went. We talked about sports and how this had fueled my competitiveness at an early age. Don shared his love for baseball, which he played at the collegiate level. Don appreciated my hard-charging, direct approach as well as why I had been hired: to reshape Nintendo by appealing to fans who wanted a return to the glory years and to use our compelling content to bring in new fans. These discussions created an extraordinary bond and high level of trust.

THE SO WHAT

Recruit advisors who can ask tough questions and push you outside of your comfort zone. Subordinates are often trying to impress you, and it is the rare one who will push back on your ideas. Outside confidants will tell you the way things are, not the way you want them to be. This is a critical perspective. Cultivate advisors—and staff—who are strong minded and confident enough to challenge your thinking.

I felt comfortable sharing with Don all my ideas as well as key information on new products in development. This was a breach in protocol. In the past, product information was very closely held. But I received support from Mike Fukuda—and eventually Mr. Iwata—that in order to create effective plans and messaging, I needed to share information early with a limited number of key people. And Don Varyu was on that list.

FAMOUS FIRST WORDS

With three months until E3 2004, Don and I were shaping the overall messaging arc for our key events: a morning press conference followed by a presentation and hospitality event for retailers in the late afternoon. We knew that we had strong content to share with new games in the *Metroid Prime*, *Star Fox* and *Paper Mario* franchises, as well as strong content from our partners like *Resident Evil 4* and *Killer 7* published by Capcom. At this point, I had also seen a top-secret trailer that our product development team—called the Treehouse—was working on directly with developers from Kyoto for the next *Legend of Zelda* game. And we had the unveiling of the Nintendo DS.

Learning from the strengths and weaknesses of past press conferences, we created an overall theme for every phase of our E3 activity and focused on the games. This was always where Nintendo shone brightest. But we also upped the competitiveness, taking the other console manufacturers head on by proclaiming Nintendo made games worth playing.

And we had me. This was to be my first major presentation as the new EVP of sales and marketing.

Don pitched me on my opening lines of the conference: "My name is Reggie. I'm about kicking ass and taking names. And I'm about making games!" At the time, I didn't know these lines would become a rallying cry among our players and a key moment in E3 history. All I knew was that the line captured the aggressive and disruptive attitude characterizing our stellar lineup of games. It foretold our innovative path with the Nintendo DS. It signaled that this was a new chapter for Nintendo.

I loved the lines, but I pushed back and challenged them. My job was to play devil's advocate because I knew they would be challenged by the executives in Kyoto. We all agreed that Nintendo needed to be more aggressive. We knew we had the pipeline of products to support the tone. But this message was clearly catering to media and players outside of Japan. I would need to convince Mr. Iwata that the message was right for our global audience, including Japan, and gain his support. While I began this salesmanship via emails with Mr. Iwata, I recognized that an upcoming face-to-face meeting would be key. Sitting together, I might be able to convince him on this approach.

Traveling to NOA's Redmond headquarters with Mr. Iwata was his key translator and our contact on PR-related matters, Mr. Yasuhiro Minagawa. I had met Mr. Minagawa on my first trip to Kyoto. He spoke perfect English and had acted as Howard Lincoln's personal translator when he had business meetings with Mr. Hiroshi Yamauchi, past president of Nintendo and great-grandson of its founder. In fact, at the time, Mr. Minagawa was still working with Howard and Mr. Yamauchi on business dealings with the Seattle Mariners, where Mr. Yamauchi was the largest shareholder and Howard was the team's CEO. Mr. Minagawa and I would become dear friends, enjoying sake and Japanese delicacies while in Tokyo, and red wine and great meals while together in the West.

THE PIVOTAL MEETING

When Mr. Iwata and Mr. Minagawa arrived in town from Kyoto, we sat down in a NOA conference room to discuss the upcoming E3. I set up the conversation by reemphasizing the objective to engage with our existing Nintendo audience as well as broadening our message to other gamers. I also emphasized that our in-person audience would be gaming media who were already biased against Nintendo. We needed to change the conversation by being bold.

I had Don read my opening lines aloud to the group so that I would be free to study Mr. Iwata's reaction. His face was blank, but his stillness, the slight squinting of his eyes, and the furrowing of his forehead told me that he was attempting to absorb the meaning and implication of the words. The room remained silent. Mr. Minagawa said something to Mr. Iwata in Japanese; I leaned over to Mike Fukuda to get a translation.

"They don't understand it," Mike whispered. So I jumped in at this point.

"Mr. Iwata, from our very first conversation you were clear that Nintendo needed to change the conversation with our business partners and with our fans. We need to be clear that we are focused on driving the industry. We are going to be aggressive. We will drive innovation. We will look to be successful across the world, recognizing that 75 percent of all gaming revenue is done outside of Japan. This line is the opening phase of our new direction."

Mr. Minagawa was translating all of this into Japanese for Mr. Iwata, even though we all knew Mr. Iwata understood English. He used this as a way to give himself added time to think and to understand nuances fully. Still, he remained silent after Mr. Minagawa was done.

Finally, Mr. Minagawa broke the ice. "Reggie, I have a question. Why are you so angry?"

Oh boy. I had a lot of explaining to do. "Mr. Minagawa, I am not saying this in anger. I am saying this with a conviction that Nintendo is on a new path. A different path than our competition. We need people to believe our path is correct."

"Reggie is right," Mr. Iwata finally spoke. "We are embarking on a very different path than our competitors. We have made so many industry advances for which we have not fully received credit. We need to be more aggressive in our messaging. I support this opening line."

STRESS REHEARSALS

And with his support, we moved forward. We spent the balance of the meeting discussing the key beats of our presentation.

Highlighting the momentum that Nintendo had with a fall 2003 price cut to GameCube and all the new software we were launching in late 2004 to maintain sales would be critical. We would emphasize the strength of our handheld business, first by featuring Game Boy Advance and then introducing the Nintendo DS. We would tease the launch of our next home console and referred to it as Revolution. And we would show a trailer for the *Zelda* game and have Mr. Miyamoto come out onstage.

It would be a new day for Nintendo.

Don Varyu and I wrote and rewrote every part of our E3 presentations. This was a critical reapplication of the lessons I had learned so many years prior from the Cornell professors I had worked for. For a presentation to be successful, no detail is too small to address. I had to do this in addition to all my other responsibilities, so I had many long nights and weekends at the office.

All these working hours had an upside though: members of the Treehouse were also working long hours preparing our games and game trailers for the show. This built camaraderie. I wasn't that much older than many of the staff. I was invited to join in the late-night food orders, and we talked about games while eating. These interactions boosted my cred and gave me even more insight to Nintendo and how the company thinks about games and their localization.

THE SO WHAT

Too often leaders don't spend time deep in the organization to identify the issues holding people back and to win the hearts of their teams. I believe in true "boots on the ground" leadership. This should go beyond your own reporting line and expand into every part of the company. The insights generated typically have a dramatic ability to simplify operations and drive both revenue and profit.

After weeks of rewriting and internal rehearsals, we arrived in Los Angeles in advance of the E3 presentation. As this was my first E3, I was following certain preestablished Nintendo protocols. For example, the media presentation was to be done in the ballroom of the Loews Hotel. Given the excitement we were looking to create, it was a fairly drab venue. On the other hand, the retail and business-partner presentation was to be executed in the grand Kodak (now Dolby) Theatre—the home of the Academy Awards since the theater opened a couple of years prior.

Another odd protocol was that I was given the largest suite in the hotel, with a grand piano and sweeping views of the city, while Mr. Iwata was placed in a very nice but much smaller suite. I had challenged this many times, pushing for Mr. Iwata to be in the best room in the hotel. But the past EVP of sales and marketing had always insisted on the best room wherever he stayed, and now I was grandfathered into this rule. Mr. Iwata was gracious about this and had me stay in this spectacular suite. I did make a point to frequently invite him to the room for breakfast so we would continue to build our relationship. I also had a dinner organized for the senior developers from Japan and members of my team. I was surprised that this form of relationship building did not exist in a meaningful way before my arrival at Nintendo. To me, building personal relationships is an important foundation for having strong business relationships. Understanding motivations and perspectives can help bridge disagreements and lead to better overall solutions.

RELEARNING THE LINES

On-site, we practiced the presentation many times. We wanted everyone to deliver the best performance they could. During these practice sessions, we became concerned about my opening lines. Not the kicking ass and taking names part—that was working perfectly.

But the next line—"I'm about making games"—was off. I was not a developer. I didn't write code or create grand visions for games. I was a businessman, a marketer. The line was not working.

The day before the presentation, I met with Perrin Kaplan, my head of communications. She said, "Reggie, the line is not working and many of us are getting uncomfortable." Initially, Perrin wanted to scrap the entire opening and write something else. I pulled Don Varyu into this impromptu meeting, and we began to exchange ideas.

"Perrin, we are not going to scrap the entire opening just because I am not a game developer. We need to find a different solution," I said.

Don said: "Guys, this is easy. We just need to tweak the end. It's not that Reggie is making the games, it's that *Nintendo* is making the games. Nintendo and all our business partners. It is 'we' in the total sense. We're about making games."

So, the night before E3 2004, we wordsmithed my opening line and changed it to the iconic phrase: "My name is Reggie. I'm about kicking ass. I'm about taking names. And *we're* about making games."

THE SO WHAT

When you are under the microscope as a leader and when a particular presentation's impact will be magnified, every word counts. Don't underestimate the impact of your words; a pronoun can make the difference between success and failure.

MOMENT OF TRUTH

The morning of the presentation, I was incredibly calm. I was confident in my command of the material, even though I was to deliver the vast majority of the fifty-minute press conference. Once I arrived at the venue, I saw members of the press already lining up to get in. At this point, nobody knew who I was, so I just walked past the line. As doors opened and the room began to fill, I went to the side of our stage and looked out over the crowd to feed off their energy. I was in a gray suit with a black T-shirt underneath—typical techie executive attire. I had already taken off my credentials that provided access to this area, and we still had members of our crew getting everything ready. One young man passed by me a couple of times, glancing over his shoulder nervously. I just stood there, looking over the crowd and then looking him over. He stopped midstride. "Hey, it's okay. Here is my badge." He thought I was the security guard! I laughed this off, but years later I would wonder what it said about the video game industry that a Black man in a suit was mistaken for security versus an executive.

THE SO WHAT

Being "different" causes a reaction. Gender, orientation, race, disability . . . the list is long. You can't ignore or avoid this reaction. Instead, lean into it. Don't hide, deny, or moderate who you are. Authenticity earns respect. So be your authentic self.

BIRTH OF THE REGGINATOR

It was time. A theatrical video opened our event, with quick-cut visuals from highly anticipated games with throbbing music underneath. The music built to a crescendo, and the video ended with our mantra for the week: "We make games worth playing." I had been standing onstage in the dark during the video, and then the lights came up full force. The crowd was cheering for the video as I stood on the stage and calmly panned over the room.

I stood in the center of the stage, and as initial camera flashes popped, I said the opening lines. We cut away to more trailers and music for a couple of minutes, then the lights came back up for me to deliver the next stanza. Now the crowd's applause was louder. As the presentation continued, we gained more applause, and video lights were on constantly as the media outlets decided they wanted to capture every moment of our presentation.

Later in the presentation, camera flashes went off like a string of firecrackers when I showed the Nintendo DS to the world for the very first time. The *Zelda* trailer, too, was a huge hit. Media representatives actually cried with joy at the look of a more mature Link and the exciting game play. Mr. Miyamoto came out onstage with a sword and shield from the game, and the crowd absolutely lost their mind.

After the presentation was over, we had a number of quick interviews and a photo op with Mr. Iwata and me holding the Nintendo DS. Then we had a quick break for lunch and prep for the business partner conference that I would deliver in just a few hours. During this break, I received a message from my younger son—the one who had beaten *Super Street Fighter* at age three. He was now fourteen and an avid gamer himself. He was familiar with all the gaming websites, including the ones that were too small or edgy to be part of Nintendo's press focus. He sent me a number of images from the press conference, all with positive commentary about the event. I decided to call him to find out where he was seeing this.

"Dad," my son said, "you're famous!" Fans were photoshopping pictures of me from the press conference and adding effects such as laser beams from my eyes and weapons in my hands to characterize my aggressive statements and the new energy from Nintendo. The Nintendo fan base must have had an affinity for Arnold Schwarzenegger's blockbuster *Terminator* franchise because they riffed on it to give me a new nickname—The Regginator.

But immediately following the press conference, Perrin and her team had not shared any early reaction, so this was the first feedback I received. I gave my son a project—to collect links for all the articles he was seeing and to send them to me. Just before I headed to the Kodak Theatre, I sent a note to Perrin with all the links. My son's work led to the creation of a new process for real-time monitoring of our press events and announcements. We had to work at internet speed given the burgeoning interest in video games, and Nintendo in particular.

BRINGING IN CUSTOMERS AND CUSTOMS

A number of other new processes and traditions came out from my first E3. I had pushed for an increased attention to detail for the hospitality event that followed our business partner presentation. We increased the prestige of the musical talent that would play at the event. My first year we had Sheryl Crow; later we would have Maroon 5 right after their Best New Artist Grammy, and also the Black Eyed Peas. I had the team create a VIP area with limited access, which was very contentious. Senior leaders from other departments felt they, and their own business partners, were somehow receiving inferior treatment. But I explained that it was important to have an area where all the executives would be located, so that staff could bring guests to us for quick conversations versus aimlessly wandering and hoping to bump into an important partner.

While these moves may seem minor, they were critical to my teaching approach. I wanted every member of my team to think deeply about their area of responsibility and always be driving improvements. They needed to learn "best in class" implementation from other companies and apply them to our situation at NOA. And I hoped to rid them of the "that's the way we have always done it" mentality. It just wasn't good enough; we had to make sure our approach was right for the current moment.

The last of the new traditions would occur on the final evening of E3. I would leverage the big suite to host a party. Initially, this started as a "thank you" to members of my sales/marketing team, our agency partners, and my fellow executives. I also invited members of Nintendo from Japan and other subsidiaries in town for E3. Over the years this would include other key department staff and would become too big for my room to accommodate.

I knew how hard everyone was working to execute E3 flawlessly. And while I didn't know in advance how media and our business partners would react, I assumed success and was ready to thank the team. I brought with me a number of lapel pins featuring our iconic characters and little note cards on which I could write personal messages to single out members of my team and recognize them for above and beyond performance. I gave one pin to a manager in our marketing team who worked on the retail meeting and hospitality event. She had to make the biggest shift from the old paradigm of repeating the same uninspired legacy tactics to my way of working. She was shocked when I publicly recognized her in front of the gathered group. Afterward, with a tear in her eye, she thanked me for the positive words in my note. "Kelley," I said. "No, thank you for trusting me with the new direction and working so hard to make it happen. You are a model for where we are going." She was super motivated in all her work from that moment on. And so, another tradition—Reggie Pins—was born.

These efforts proved to be transformative for Nintendo. Previously the company had been very siloed. The three geographic regions—NCL managing Asia, NOE responsible for Europe, and NOA—tended not to share plans or best practices. There was an undercurrent of competition among the regions. I had a different perspective. I wanted to learn from the other regions, reapplying their best ideas and avoiding their mistakes. I valued personal relationships in order to foster trust and straight talk.

Reggie Pins, and importantly the handwritten notes that accompanied them, provided a personal reward for a job well done. Handing these out in the public forum of a celebratory event was icing on the cake for the recipients. This recognition drove team members to try harder and achieve more.

THE SO WHAT

No idea is ever totally new. Steal and reapply. My focus on observing other regions in my company as well as my competitors began during my earliest days at P&G. I would take good ideas, add my own twist or unique element, and apply it to my own business. Same is true with personal notes to reward performance . . . the best managers I ever had did this.

11

DRIVING A VISION

My first E3 and the unveiling of the Nintendo DS was a success, but we had a few issues to resolve.

We received harsh feedback on the prototype DS units we showed at the event. People perceived the design to be clunky and cheap. The screens where described as small and the images weren't crisp. The criticism was especially tough because a prototype of the PlayStation Portable was also at E3 2004. Their unit was essentially one large screen and looked beautiful. It didn't matter that the screen would be covered with fingerprints or potentially crack in the real world. In the enclosed space of E3, attendees would handle the unit for a minute and then gingerly hand it back to a Sony representative, who would immediately wipe it down to remove fingerprints.

While we had described the Nintendo DS software as proof-of-concept demos, booth attendees were evaluating them as full-fledged games. This became a key area of messaging focus for us. We had to reinforce the point that these were only examples of what could be done with a game, whether the stylus was used for targeting by touching the screen, or if action could be manipulated by blowing on the system's microphone. Most of the media understood our messaging, but many others did not and complained aggressively.

We needed to step up the pace of our activity in order to deliver on our promise to achieve our goals.

METROID PRIME HUNTERS EXPLODES

Within two months, we tweaked the physical design of the DS. We showed it off to the world and received a vastly improved reception.

Behind the scenes, I was lobbying for the Americas to launch the system first so we could leverage Black Friday—the day after Thanksgiving in the US and the biggest shopping day of the year. We would need the largest production allocation of all the regions if we launched first. Both of these launch plan elements were unheard of as Japan always launched systems first and received preferential production allocation until demand trends were clear.

I pulled together the sales and marketing team to review our launch plans. I challenged every phase and made sure that our plans were right for the present conditions and not predicated on old ways of working. For example, I introduced a planning tactic for our teams to challenge every retailer to give us their support plans and made it clear that we would reward more aggressive activity with more launch inventory. This was different from old thinking that simply allocated inventory based on current market share. My new approach encouraged disruption by retailers betting on our success with their own marketing activity.

All of these new approaches were risky. But I wanted the first new product launch under my leadership to be an unqualified success. I pushed the internal teams hard.

I also pushed our parent company hard. My message to Mr. Iwata was straighforward: if we wanted Nintendo DS to be a global success, it first needed to be a success in the Americas.

We pushed the development team to finish up a key game for our market called *Metroid Prime Hunters*. This was a first-person shooting-style game that enabled up to four players to compete wirelessly. *Metroid Prime* had been a strong-selling franchise on Game-Cube in our market, and leveraging the franchise to launch Nintendo

DS would help us get off to a fast start. Unfortunately, development was not proceeding as fast as we hoped. So I advocated an alternative: the development team should pivot and create a stand-alone demo that we would include with the first units of Nintendo DS hardware. This was controversial, as our developers hated to give content away for free. And having the development team work on a demo would push the launch of the complete game back at least six months.

I was already building trust with Mr. Iwata and Mr. Miyamoto, and they agreed for a demo called *Metroid Prime Hunters: First Hunt* to be included in the first few million units of Nintendo DS sold in the Americas. And Nintendo DS launched first in the Americas. As a result, during November and December 2004, more than one million units were sold in the US alone, and in January 2005, Nintendo reported global shipments of Nintendo DS had exceeded expectations.

THE SO WHAT

Pushing yourself and others hard is critical to achieving superior results. Ask for the innovative twist or for an idea that has never been done before in your industry—but is common elsewhere. You can't be afraid of being overaggressive in your asks when a lot is riding on the outcome.

But it starts with your own personal behavior. When others see how hard you are pushing yourself and how high you have set your own standards, they are much more willing to deliver on your demands.

START OF A REVOLUTION

While the positive early sales were a strong boost of confidence, we were playing a long game. We wanted Nintendo DS, and our next home console, code-named Revolution, to bring gaming to a mass audience and increase the number of people playing video games globally.

Our belief was that game innovation had stalled and other companies were bringing out rehashed versions of prior games. And we felt that input devices—the controllers used to move your character through gaming enviromnents—had become too complicated. Our own GameCube controller had eleven different buttons and triggers, including two analog sticks and one directional-pad.

This is why DS included a more streamlined button layout, a touchscreen, and a mic for voice commands. And this is why Mr. Miyamoto and his team were hard at work on a game that would fully use these capabilities in a truly innovative way.

The new game was a radical idea at the time: a pet simulator called *Nintendogs*. There was no scoring objective and no set progression; the game only had you name and raise a pet dog, interacting with it as you chose. This was completely different from sports, shooting, or adventure-style games. It was experiential and unstructured. And it was a ton of fun, especially for girls and young women.

Remembering the problems we had earlier at E3, when we had not been clear enough about how players should experience our games, we challenged ourselves to come up with a clear and compelling communication plan for our unorthodox approach. We needed to make sure all our constituents—the media, the financial analysts, the big game developers like Activision and EA, our players/fans, as well as our own employees—understood our thinking. Without this, there would be significant negative reaction that might derail us.

BOOK LEARNING

We decided to use principles from a couple of popular business books to help constituents understand our plans. Both Mr. Iwata and I were voracious readers, and we compared notes to find effective theories that helped to dramatize our approach.

The first book we agreed to use was *The Innovator's Dilemma* by Clayton Christensen. Christensen wrote that businesses need to constantly reevaluate whether to continue along their existing path that caters to current customer needs or adopt new approaches that meet future and maybe unarticulated needs. This fit well with the gaming industry as both PlayStation and Xbox were pushing on traditional vectors: more realistic visuals supported by increased processing power. Nintendo believed this was a dead end. More realistic visuals by themselves did not result in a better game. And more processing power would lead to higher costs and higher consumer prices, which would limit the potential market versus expanding it.

Instead, if Nintendo innovated along other vectors, such as ease of game play or increased accessibility, we could fundamentally change the market. This approach would leave our competitors in a difficult position of having to catch up to us along a vector they were ill-equipped to compete in.

The other book we agreed to use was *Blue Ocean Strategy* by W. Chan Kim and Renée Mauborgne. The core idea was that it is more profitable for companies to avoid overdeveloped and saturated markets ("red oceans") and instead to pivot to "blue oceans" in uncontested and growing markets. This summarized Nintendo's focus at the time: creating games appealing to nontraditional players, such as girls or players over fifty. This theory dovetailed with *The Innovator's Dilemma*, and the combined ideas provided an understandable framework for our approach.

THE SO WHAT

When embarking on a new direction, leaders must overcommunicate to all their constituents. Everyone needs to

understand your direction. Analogies and historical examples can
be powerful elements in your communication.

You will also have to repeat yourself and at times convey the
same message in different ways. Repetition drives understanding.

I incorporated both books and their business theories into my
press interviews and financial analyst meetings. We gave away copies
and encouraged our business partners to read them. I got into debates
with members of the gaming press who used other business books
to support our competitors' tactics. I even received fan letters thank-
ing me for using *The Innovator's Dilemma* and *Blue Ocean Strategy* to
explain our approach and asking for other recommendations to read.

The launch of *Nintendogs* paid off our messaging roadshow. The
game was completely different from anything before it. And it sold
exceptionally well worldwide, expanding Nintendo's base to include
younger kids and girls. It remains the second highest-selling game
on the Nintendo DS and won many prestigious awards, including
the Best Handheld Game from the Associated Press in 2006. Our
strategy was further exemplified by the launch of *Brain Age* for the
Nintendo DS and with the unveiling of our next home console.

12

INTERNAL DISRUPTION

The development and launch of *Brain Age* marked the next phase of my time at Nintendo when I more aggressively pushed for initiatives that would drive results across all the company's Western markets. By mid-2005, Nintendo DS was doing well globally. But the Western markets—Europe, Australia, plus my region of US/Canada/Mexico/Central and South America—were not performing as strongly as Japan on a per capita basis. I used this fact to drive Nintendo of America. I communicated internally to our teams the relative lack of performance and challenged the sales and marketing teams to improve every facet of our go-to-market strategy.

BRAINSTORM

The heart of the issue was that once we had launched *Nintendogs*, our pipeline of new and innovative software was weak for the Western markets. In Japan, a number of unique and innovative games had launched, leveraging DS's touchscreen and targeting new audiences. But none of these games had been localized for the key Western languages or made much of a sales impact in the West.

Brain Age, launched in spring 2005, was different and had a lasting impact on DS hardware sales in Japan. The game used the touchscreen and microphone to solve puzzles. You would test yourself with these rotating puzzles daily and receive a brain "age" with the objective to lower this age with continued use of the software. *Brain Age* was based on the work of Dr. Ryuta Kawashima, a neurophysiologist who was teaching and conducting experiments at Tohoku University in Japan. His research led to bestselling books in Japan highlighting his brain age theory and a variety of puzzles.

Development of Nintendo's *Brain Age* game was a direct result of Mr. Iwata and Dr. Kawashima brainstorming ideas on how to use the professor's theory in a video game. The game was developed in less than five months and launched in Japan on May 19, 2005.

Beyond its use of puzzles, math, reading aloud, and other non-fun activities in a video game, the software and its results were unique in a variety of ways.

The initial allocation of software to retailers sold through quickly. As Nintendo worked with Japanese retailers to restock the software, sales grew. This was very unusual. Japan is noted for being a trend-driven market, and you can go from hot to cold in a matter of weeks. After a video game software is initially launched, sales typically decline rapidly over time. Rarely do they grow, other than with the seasonal buying bump of a holiday. *Brain Age* was showing a very different sales pattern. Throughout its initial launch, the game stayed as a weekly top-ten-selling industry title, despite DS hardware having just been launched and it being a very different sort of game experience.

The game was also targeting a nontraditional video game audience: consumers over the age of fifty. These consumers likely didn't own a Nintendo DS themselves. They would need to borrow their child's or grandchild's device to experience the game. Later, should they continue using the software, they would need to invest in the hardware for their own use, which would be a significant purchase. But this is exactly what happened in the Japanese market. Stories immediately surfaced of kids being frustrated that their parents were using the DS all the time. It was the children who insisted that their parents buy their own DS to continue enjoying *Brain Age*.

LOCAL RELEVANCE

Excited by the results, Mr. Iwata and I discussed how to localize the game for our market. There were many challenges. First, there were no existing models for recognizing Western handwriting. Japan as a culture is quite homogeneous, so the writing recognition tool set created for their market was quick to build. But in the West, the handwriting for numerals varies widely. Do your own test: write the numerals 3, 4, 5, and 8 on a piece of paper. Then watch your family members and friends write the same numerals. Observe the pen-strokes and look at the variations in how the numerals are shaped. In our play testing at Nintendo of America, we saw a vast range. We would need to build a proprietary tool set for the software to recognize the variety of handwritten numerals quickly, as speed was a key element of the brain testing.

We had to do the same for voice recognition as there was a module in the original *Brain Age* software from Japan that had the player reading aloud. Another challenge for Western markets was the number of languages. In my region alone, we needed English, Spanish, Québecois French, and Brazilian Portugese. Many more languages were needed for the European business. Localizing the software for all these languages would take time.

SOLVING THE PUZZLE

But the biggest issue was making *Brain Age* relevant for our consumer. In Japan, Dr. Kawashima and his principles were very well known. Nintendo had leveraged this by including his name in marketing materials and using a blocky version of his head as the character conducting tutorials and interacting with the player within the game itself. We had none of this relevance outside of Japan.

What was gaining in popularity in our market, however, was sudoku, the number placement puzzle. Sudoku puzzles were appearing next to crossword puzzles in leading newspapers, and dedicated sudoku puzzle books were becoming bestsellers. Many people also believed solving sudoku puzzles improved memory. And they were incredibly popular with older consumers in the West.

I talked to Mr. Iwata about including sudoku in the Western version of *Brain Age*.

"Mr. Iwata, I have concerns about the appeal of *Brain Age* in our market," I started. "Dr. Kawashima is unknown in the West, and in Japan you were able to very successfully use his prior work to establish awareness of *Brain Age* software. We will not have that benefit. Also, culturally, you had benefits in Japan that we will not have. There is a much larger percentage of the population that is over fifty years old in Japan. In the US and Canada, and especially in my region's markets in Latin America, the demographics are very different. Ours is a much younger population. We will need to think about this software differently in our markets.

"I would like to add sudoku to the software as we localize it for the West. Sudoku is very trendy, and playing this math puzzle is popular with our older target audience. But it also has the ability to reach younger adults as they are playing these puzzles as well."

Immediately, Mr. Iwata pushed back. "Reggie, *Brain Age* is based on Dr. Kawashima's work. We spent a great deal of time getting him comfortable with the activities we designed from the inspiration of his books. I am not sure he ever used sudoku in his research. It will be challenging to do what you propose."

I could tell this was personally difficult for Mr. Iwata. He was the one who had initially met with Dr. Kawashima about the idea. I was sure he had been involved in the delicate negotiations concerning how Nintendo was representing the brain age concept. After just a couple of years working with Mr. Iwata, I knew that when he stopped smiling and had longer pauses before reacting to an idea that he was getting uncomfortable. But I pressed on.

"Mr. Iwata, research materials about sudoku are very consistent with Dr. Kawashima's principles. Focused and short-duration exercises seem to improve memory. If we expose him to the idea, and why we believe it makes sense for the West, I hope he would see the benefit."

It was a compelling argument, and I could aleady sense Mr. Iwata had moved past consideration of the idea and on to how he would engage Dr. Kawashima to gain his support.

I had learned that it was foolish to push for a firm decision at an initial review of an idea. I needed to let Mr. Iwata continue to think about the idea on his own. But when we would have our regular communication by email and videoconference, I would always ask about sudoku and how conversations were going with Dr. Kawashima.

I also knew I needed to push the idea from other angles. I worked with Mike Fukuda to gain his support as he and his team would be working directly with the NCL developers. They also needed to buy into the idea and then begin to work on how best to integrate this new element into the software that already had been launched in Japan. New menus and tutorials would need to be created to make sudoku feel integral to the software, versus a "bolt-on" set of activities.

Mike's team would also need to source the content. NOA didn't have sudoku puzzles lying around.

I also worked with our legal team to understand any copyright or trademark issues around sudoku. This was a new area for us, and we needed to educate ourselves quickly.

Within a few weeks, we had the answer from Mr. Iwata: Dr. Kawashima enthusiastically endorsed the addition of sudoku. The NCL developers were excited about the idea as well, as they, too, had been concerned about how to make the software as compelling as possible in the West.

THE SO WHAT

When selling a new or provocative idea, you need allies. Pushing the idea from multiple angles improves the chance that the ultimate decision-maker will support the initiative. And when you are the ultimate decision-maker and a number of your subordinates are advocating for an idea, know that they have been discussing it and aligning on it. This is a good thing.

GAMING FOR THE MASSES

We solved the handwriting and voice command issues, seamlessly integrated sudoku, and launched the software in April 2006. Just as in the Japanese market, we saw initial sales that were steady, but they continued to grow month by month. More importantly, the software was associated with the purchase of new hardware. We were achieving our objective to expand the gaming universe.

While we were creating momentum for the Nintendo DS, we were also hard at work on our next home console. We were deliberate in our messaging. We publicly referred to the system as Revolution, refering to the revolution in game play that we were hoping to achieve. For the Nintendo fan, we messaged an important feature of the new system: the ability to play previously released games from the NES and SNES generation via a digital "virtual console" capable of downloading these games.

We decided to reveal the new system's controller at the 2005 Tokyo Game Show. Because we wanted everyone in the household to be comfortable playing games on our upcoming system, we designed the controller to resemble a flat, oblong TV remote. You could pick it up and play with either hand.

Our controller had motion sensing and gyroscopic technology, meaning that by swinging or pointing the remote you facilitated game play. We limited the buttons to make the controller accessible. For more complicated software catering to the experienced gamer, attachments with a joystick and added buttons were available to provide more functionality.

At the Tokyo Game Show, all we did was talk about the controller and display a few still pictures of it, but we captured everyone's imagination about the possibilities for new software experiences.

I returned to Japan later in 2005 to continue work on our messaging and rollout of Revolution. Internally, we were making sure that the pace of our public messaging kept our audience engaged, but we wanted to hold significant surprises for E3 in May 2006.

We agreed that Mr. Iwata would make another keynote address at the Game Developers Conference (GDC) in March 2006. He had given a very successful speech the year prior, titled "Heart of a Gamer" where he told personal stories about his path to becoming president of Nintendo but how in his heart he would always be a gamer. The construct for this speech had been very similar to my "Kicking Ass" speech: Mr. Iwata spent many hours with Don Varyu to communicate his background and motivations. I sat in on a few of these interviews, and it was a good thing.

We had a scare during preparations: Mr. Iwata developed a bad case of laryngitis. The day before he was scheduled to speak, he had hardly any voice at all. Don and I were frantically going through backup plans should this continue and Mr. Iwata not be able to speak. We kicked around the idea that I would have to deliver the speech for him, with Mr. Iwata there onstage. I would be a sort of ventriloquist's dummy, saying the words about a personal history that wasn't mine. I spent all night reading the speech, thinking about how I would need to tailor it in real time to pull this magic trick off. Luckily, Mr. Iwata recovered enough to deliver the speech. It was probably the best speech he ever delivered in English.

THE STORY BEHIND WII

During GDC 2006, we used the success of *Brain Age* to reinforce how Nintendo was approaching the market differently. For Revolution, we went further behind the scenes to explain the development of the new controller and how it would create opportunities for our business partners to bring their content to life.

A couple of months after GDC, we unveiled the name of our new system. We wanted a name that could be said in any language— further testimony to our goal of expanding gaming to as many consumers as possible. Wii was announced. Pronounced "we," the name was a concerted effort to highlight the inclusive nature of our approach. We anticipated that some would make jokes based on this name (Wii, wee-wee). But the distinctive term combined with its inclusiveness made the naming decision worth it.

E3 2006 would be where we culminated our messaging. We would showcase the games Nintendo and our partners were working on for both the Nintendo DS and for Wii. We would have them available for all sixty thousand show attendees to play. This would be a particular challenge because we had a ton of games to show, and our traditional booth size was too small. This was especially true because we needed to have more space between players as some Wii games required swinging our new remote like a tennis racket or baseball bat. We also had experiences mandating multiple players side by side. So we took a large amount of space adjacent to our booth and made this a dedicated showcase for Wii games.

While we had an extensive line-up, two main games would drive our messaging: *Wii Sports*, a collection of five sports experiences that you played with your own avatar—your Mii; and *The Legend of Zelda: Twilight Princess*, the fully developed game we had teased at E3 2004.

Wii Sports was designed to be played by everyone. The combination of baseball, tennis, boxing, golf, and bowling promised global appeal. Software preloaded to every Wii console took you through a creation process where you would make your Mii, choosing between a variety of options for skin tone, height, weight, hair, facial expressions, and eye color. Then in the *Wii Sports* software, you would play sports games either against your friends' Miis or an AI Mii. The game was deliberately straightforward but led to animated competitions, even among Nintendo staff as they were developing the game. We knew it would be a great way to showcase the capabilities of Wii to span generations and have everyone picking up the controller.

KEEPING FANS IN THE GAME

The Legend of Zelda: Twilight Princess was very different. It was a traditional *Zelda* game, where you navigated the hero, Link, to fight enemies and solve puzzles. Your quest was to save Princess Zelda and the Hyrule world. This game was for the traditional Nintendo gamer audience. We also knew this game would sell exceptionally well.

Internally, we had intense debates about how to prioritize these games within our conferences and overall at E3. They played different roles.

Wii Sports was peak innovation: a completely new experience that would motivate a wide range of people, including those new to games, to pick up a controller and play.

Zelda would be the must-have game for our current fans and a major profit driver for our retailers. Importantly, *Zelda* would show the big game developers like Activision and EA that they could be successful on our platform with traditional action, sports, and shooting-style games that catered to the core audience.

In the end, Mr. Iwata and I agreed that for the press conference we would put *Wii Sports* in the coveted position of closing the event. We ran a contest offering a US consumer the opportunity to be the first to play the game on our stage. The lucky winner would join Mr. Miyamoto, Mr. Iwata, and me to play *Wii Sports* tennis. Executing a big *Wii Sports* finale would ensure we reached the global audience watching online with our innovation.

For the retailer presentation, we would conclude the event with *The Legend of Zelda*. It was a known franchise, and retailers would be excited about the revenue and profit potential.

We had other surprises for the press conference. We opened the conference with Mr. Miyamoto in a full tuxedo and tails conducting an orchestra of Miis. He transitioned from conducting the Miis to "conducting" demonstrations of new games from Nintendo and from our licensee partners. It was classic Mr. Miyamoto with his big smile and big personality. He handed the presentation to me, and I went through our full pitch for Wii and Nintendo DS. Overall, the presentation was a huge hit.

DOING THE RIGHT THING

So huge that after the press conference, Mr. Iwata sent word to me that he wanted to change the retailer presentation at the last minute to have it flow the same as the press presentation. This would mean a shorter demo for *Zelda* earlier in the flow of the presentation and a longer *Wii Sports* demo onstage to conclude the event.

My concern with this late potential change was twofold. First, I fundamentally believed we would get a better reaction from our retailers with *Zelda* as the closing reveal. These were executives that largely focused only on the bottom line. They wanted only to make money on the hardware, software, and accessories we sold to them and they, in turn, sold to consumers. While it was important for them to understand and ideally support our strategy, they would push what they knew worked best for them. *Zelda*, as a big franchise with millions of fans, did that.

Second, the magnitude of change that Mr. Iwata was advocating for in our presentation was significant. These were heavily produced events, with lighting, sound, and scripts—any of which could fail with a late change that had never been rehearsed.

I found Mr. Iwata and met with him privately to review his demand. "Mr. Iwata, I understand you want to change the order of *Wii Sports* and *Zelda* in the upcoming retailer presentation."

"Yes, Reggie," he said. "The reaction to our press presentation has been very strong. We are generating significant excitement for Wii. To get our retailers similarly excited, we should give them the same presentation."

"Mr. Iwata, you are right that we had a very strong press briefing. *Wii Sports* is a magical game, and we will continue to get even more positive reactions as show attendees play for themselves. But as we have discussed, retailers' needs are different. They are looking at our lineup and making decisions on how much Wii hardware to order, as well as which individual games to support. *Zelda* is a known hardware seller. Retailers need to see significant potential in this title. We really covered it only briefly in the press event because media are familiar with the franchise. They are already sold on the game. For retailers, they need to see more.

"Also, Mr. Iwata, making a change at this point, only a couple of hours before we go onstage, is a recipe for disaster. We cannot ruin our effort with technical difficulties. The right thing to do is to stay with our plan."

We did our typical dance. Back and forth, making sure we heard each other's point of view but offering real objections and real risks on our positions. And the longer the discussion continued, the higher the executional risk grew. In the end, he relented and we stayed with our original plan. But in this case, I felt Mr. Iwata was a little disappointed in me. I believe he hoped I would just say yes and honor his request as our global president. But I needed to do what was right for the business—and right for my organization. Driving understanding of the *Zelda* game was critically important to our market. If retailers were excited for this game, it would drive excitement for the Wii console.

Also, the success of *Zelda* was important in garnering support from Western developers. They needed to believe there was an audience for their style of games on the Wii platform. They wanted a male, young-adult consumer ready for the next sports or action game they would launch to already own the Wii. A successful *Zelda* game would accomplish this.

Making significant changes to an integrated presentation a couple of hours before the scheduled start was a sure recipe for failure. My team and I would be blamed if this happened—no one would remember who had asked for the changes.

I was convinced the flow of the presentation would work for the retailers. They were seeing positive online buzz for *Wii Sports* from our earlier press presentation. They were also seeing fan commentary that had hoped for more information on the *Zelda* game, and this drove speculation about the quality of the game and whether it would really be ready at the launch of Wii.

THE SO WHAT

Leaders do the hard things. It would have been easy to defer to my boss, but I knew what was right for the situation. I held my ground, even with a risk to the relationship with my boss and to my position within the company.

When confronted with a hard decision, dig deep into your experiences, learnings, and beliefs. You need to consider the risks—the risk of going with the consensus or pushing an alternative point of view.

Then you make the tough call.

EVERYTHING CHANGES

It worked. By going into more depth with the retailers and highlighting our expectation that nearly every initial buyer of the hardware would also buy the *Zelda* game, retailers asked us for large initial allocations of both—exceeding even our own most optimistic estimates.

On the Saturday Mr. Iwata was to fly back to Japan, I had breakfast with him and shared retailer and consumer reaction to all our E3 activities. "Mr. Iwata, there is no doubt we achieved our objectives. There is video circulating on all the gaming sites showing show attendees rushing to our booth as soon as E3 doors opened yesterday."

That Friday there had been lines forming outside the E3 entry hours before doors were to open. Officially badged attendees would often give away—or sell—their badge for the last day of the show. At this point official attendees would have seen all the products they wanted and were in a hurry to get home. Game fans and retail associates from nearby electronics and video game stores would approach E3 attendees on Thursday evening as they were leaving the show to try to obtain a badge for the last day.

"In one version of this 'mad rush video,' fans go right by the PlayStation booth without stopping," I continued. "They go right to the Nintendo booth and begin lining up to see Wii and DS. You can see Sony executives just shaking their heads in wonder!

"And, Mr. Iwata, while we are still working through plans with retailers, initial requests for Wii hardware and key software are well in excess of our high-end original estimates. We will need to review manufacturing plans with you when I visit Japan next month. But we should begin thinking about increasing production now."

Mr. Iwata nodded his head and asked some basic questions. But his mind seemed elsewhere. I couldn't help but wonder if he was still upset with me for not following his instruction and changing the sequence of *Wii Sports* and *Zelda* for the retailer presentation.

The following Monday started great. While we were exhausted from all the work of putting on a successful E3 the week prior, we were also excitedly following up on all the action items from the expo. Retailers were calling to discuss their requests for larger allocations of Wii hardware and software. They also wanted to know when we would share more detail on price and launch date. We leveraged their enthusiasm to gain more immediate support for Nintendo DS.

There were also dozens of media inquiries looking for behind-the-scenes stories on the development of Wii. The PR team evaluated all of these requests as we still needed to keep consumer interest high through the summer and fall until our holiday 2006 launch.

We also needed to put the finishing touches on our launch advertising for Wii, which we would need to film within the next few weeks.

OH MY!

Amid this frenetic activity, I was jolted by the news that Mr. Iwata would be coming back to the US later that week and he wanted to speak with me upon his arrival. This was crazy! He had just been in Los Angeles with me the entire week before. We had spent dozens of hours together, both privately and in larger group meetings. What was so new and urgent that he needed to come right back?

My mind went to a dark place. Was he really upset with me about the software order in the retailer presentation and the back-and-forth discussions we had had? Was I going to be fired because I pushed back for what I believed in? And more importantly, hadn't the flow worked?

I had been very sensitive to having our disagreements in private. Even Mr. Minagawa, his customary translator, had been absent. I did not want any potential loss of face for Mr. Iwata from our discussions.

I decided I would not accept a firing or reprimand without presenting my side. I tasked my team to pull together the definitive PowerPoint deck that showed the plan had worked. We had data summarizing how Nintendo had dominated the media conversation and consumer online engagement throughout E3 for Wii, for *Wii Sports*, and for *Zelda*. We had outperformed our historical benchmarks and outperformed competitive platforms and other games from independent developers.

We also had data showing the depth of retailer support for Wii and for Nintendo DS. I was confident this support exceeded what the other subsidiary markets were achieving.

This project turned into a detailed twenty-plus-page presentation. It was a complete defense of my recommendation to focus the press presentation on *Wii Sports* and the retailer presentation on *Zelda*. It showed I had made the right call.

Mr. Iwata arrived Friday, May 19, exactly a week after the E3 attendee rush to our booth. He came directly from the airport to

NOA headquarters and went into an interior conference room he used as an office. Typically, he would stop at a hotel first to wash up and change clothes. But not this time. Also, his office had the window blinds closed—this was a first. And I learned that after meeting with me, he was meeting with the other executive vice presidents individually and then we were meeting as a group later in the day. This was all very unusual and fed into my fear.

Mr. Kimishima, the NOA president, came for me and together we walked to Mr. Iwata's makeshift office. I had three copies of my presentation, titled "NOA's E3 Results." As we were about to enter the room, Mr. Kimishima leaned to me and said, "Reggie, it is okay." What did that mean?!

Mr. Iwata sat at the head of the table and asked me to sit to his right and had Mr. Kimishima at his left. I asked how his flight had been, but his appearance already told me that it likely had been rough. He shared there had been turbulence and that he hadn't been able to get as much sleep as he wanted. I hoped this wouldn't make the meeting bumpy as well.

As I prepared to hand out copies of my presentation, Mr. Iwata asked me to stop and instead handed me a two-page document. *Here we go,* I thought.

The subject line said, "Promotion."

I read the opening line: "I am pleased to offer you the position of President and Chief Operating Officer of Nintendo of America Inc."

All I could say was, "Oh my!"

THE SO WHAT

I often reflect on how I achieved this capstone promotion. There is no single answer. But I know this: I applied all my learning as a revenue-driving executive and as a people leader to achieve results. Delivering results draws attention and leads to increased responsibility.

I had the courage of my convictions and disrupted when necessary. Push your point of view.

And I was always authentic—the same Reggie with Mr. Iwata that I was with members of my team. Authenticity in a leader is another highly prized quality, and others will recognize and reward it.

13

COURAGEOUS DECISIONS

As president of NOA, I now had to apply the skills and strategies I had been using in the sales and marketing division across the entire company.

I needed to convince my new direct reports and previous peers that I understood their functional areas and would advocate for their initiatives. These included executives in charge of finance, technology, operations, product development, and business affairs.

I held reviews with each executive to dive deep into their business. I focused on meeting their people, especially at the vice president and director levels, as these would be the potential future leaders of the company. I needed to understand where we had bench strength, and where we did not, to make sure we were well positioned for the future. I also asked questions to challenge the existing priorities and to make sure I supported the key work being done.

Throughout these meetings across the company, I focused on three common issues that needed immediate attention. First, Nintendo of America was highly siloed. Each division had its own set of priorities, but there was no sense of overall company priorities and no understanding of how everything fit together. This was a legacy issue. Global Nintendo and NOA were each centrally managed—by Hiroshi Yamauchi in Japan and by his son-in-law Minoru Arakawa at NOA. In Japan, Mr. Yamauchi ran the show. At NOA, Mr. Arakawa made all the decisions. This led to a lack of internal communication at each organization and a lack of internal teamwork.

MICROCOSM OF WHAT WAS WRONG

A classic example of this siloed thinking was the launch of Game Boy Micro in the fall of 2005. At this point, we had already launched Nintendo DS, and our focus was on making this product a long-term success. The Game Boy Advance business was in a state of decline, and NOA was planning on closing out the line with a Black Friday promotion that would clear out all our remaining inventory. These plans were created in early 2005. Shortly thereafter, I first heard of Game Boy Micro. Members of our operations and product development teams had been aware of the Micro much earlier than I.

From my perspective, the concept of Game Boy Micro was a nonstarter. The hardware was exceptionally small. Not only were the control buttons difficult for any reasonably sized adult to manipulate, but also the screen was tiny. This ran counter to current consumer electronics trends of making screens larger. But development of this hardware had continued, and now we were forced to launch the system. "We should have talked about this long ago," I told Don James and Mike Fukuda. "We should have all agreed that this product would be a distraction for us in our market and either not introduce it here or have it terminated as a project globally. By working together we could have had a different outcome." My point was not to rebuke them—at the time we were peers. It was to identify that we were operating in silos and this made us ineffective in managing projects coming from NCL.

Game Boy Micro launched globally to lackluster results, selling fewer than a million units in its first month and fewer than two million units after four months at the end of 2005.

I used this as a teachable moment for NOA. The lesson: company leadership needed constant communication on our priorities. As president, my solution was to institute weekly meetings of the executive leadership team to review key priorities and our progress against them. Initially, there was some grumbling. "Do we really need to meet weekly?" was the common lament. No executive gets excited about the prospect of more meetings. But as soon as we started, everyone saw the benefit. The grumbling stopped, sharing of information accelerated, and we saw an immediate benefit in the pace of our initiatives.

As we would begin a new fiscal year, we would align on the upcoming year's priorities. This ensured agreement across the entire company. And I would share these priorities with Mr. Iwata to shape his thinking on the overall Nintendo priorities for the upcoming year.

THE SO WHAT

Leaders create alignment through frequent meetings, calls, and digital communication. In this age of remote work and dispersed teams, real engagement is an even higher priority.

When teams and individuals are in their own bubble, they can misalign on priorities. This is especially true if silos have developed in different functions and other groups. The only way to keep the organization moving forward without missteps is by sharing information continuously and making sure everyone is using the same playbook.

CONNECTING ACTIONS TO REWARDS

My second observation was that even though both global Nintendo and NOA had strong business cultures, we had an opportunity to clarify the behaviors we valued and how they led to advancement within the company.

Nintendo of America was an anachronism in the early 2000s. The Pacific Northwest was already becoming a hot employment market across all technology fields. Employees would typically be moving from one company to the next, improving their salary and their job titles along the way. But not at NOA. We had extraordinary tenure, with employees having been with the company about eight years on average. The fun nature of the business and the constant pace of new product launches made it enjoyable for employees to stay. But the lack of focus on individual performance and accountability for results also made it overly comfortable. Especially for weaker performers. This related back to that very first conversation with Flip Morse, the head of HR, and the lack of strategy for employee development.

As the sales and marketing division head, I had already put performance management methods in place. I demanded that all employees have their semiannual reviews completed and reviewed by department heads. I put weak performers on action plans that resulted either in their improvement or their exit from the company. This was done with a clarity for the behaviors we wanted to reinforce, as well as with compassion.

For example, I had a VP within sales and marketing who was technically brilliant but a horrible people manager. No more than a month had passed from my hiring before members of his staff were coming to me to give detailed examples of his shortcomings. As I talked to his peers in other departments, I learned that his lack of people-management skills was well known but had been overlooked because of his technical mastery.

I met with him immediately. "Look, I know you have put superior tools in place and are an expert technically. But you manage a department of thirty people. I have seen how you treat your team, and it is a problem. You don't treat them with respect, and you don't invest time to help them get better. You have to become a much more effective people manager and leader of your team, or you have no future role at the company."

He was shocked. No one had delivered this message to him so clearly. We put a plan in place to give him access to additional training, an executive coach, and we met every two weeks specifically on his people-management development. I had him share with me what he was learning from his coach and how he was implementing these new tools with his team. Separately, I met with his direct subordinates to hear about progress from their perspective.

In the end, the situation had proceeded for too long. His poor people-management behavior had calcified under years of ignorance and lack of feedback. I told him that I planned to create a different role where he would have no people-management responsibility but could continue to apply his technical capability. He left the company within weeks of my disclosure to him. His department was happy to see him go.

THE SO WHAT

Be clear in the behaviors you reward, and be swift with feedback when there is underperformance. Letting weak performers remain in an organization hurts them and their team. And it creates frustration from strong performers who wonder why they are working so hard.

Confronting people who possess great technical skills but are alienating others is probably the hardest people-management challenge. It is a calculated risk. But no individual, no matter how skilled, is worth the toxic environment they create.

Firing weak or alienating performers is a tough but essential skill that every leader must master.

I applied this same approach across the entire company as president. With my executive leadership team and our human resources group, we created a matrix of NOA Competencies across five dimensions:

1. Thought—reflecting the individual mindset we wanted our employees to have, such as continuous innovation and global perspective
2. Results—demonstrating a bias for action and achievement of planned results
3. Self—addressing how the individual conducted him- or herself with trust and adaptability
4. People—addressing collaboration and valuing differences
5. Leadership—focusing on building effective teams and driving vision

We broadly communicated these competencies and tied them directly to our performance review process. We demystified the behaviors we wanted everyone to exhibit and how progression within the company would happen. Initially, this led to an increase in employee turnover, but culture surveys showed a dramatic increase in favorability for how employees felt about their future with the company.

CLASHING CULTURES

The last observation was tension between our parent company, NCL, and NOA as the subsidiary. Japan was and continues to be very different from other markets. The population is large but in a very concentrated geographic area because of the mountains in its interior. This leads to smaller homes with less individual space but more communal areas. Many households are multigenerational, and elders are highly respected. There is much less ethnic diversity versus other developed countries. The media landscape is still concentrated in a limited number of national broadcast systems.

From a business perspective, the Japan video game market only had one direct competitor—Sony's PlayStation—while the Americas and Europe had a second strong competitor with Microsoft's Xbox. First-person shooter games were performing exceptionaly well in the West. In Japan, it was inconceivable that this content would be played on the communal TV in front of Grandma. Western markets were deep in the process of content proliferation, first with digital cable channels and then with over-the-top internet content.

As a result, NCL and NOA often had very different opinions about the future of the global games industry and how best to grow our business. As I became president of NOA, there was a feeling among the executives that Western perspectives were being ignored. This situation existed despite Western markets accounting for more than 75 percent of revenue and profit—with NOA alone making up about 50 percent of each.

My approach was to ramp up the communication with NCL across every part of our business. Finance-oriented discussions. Discussions about our technical infrastructure and digital business. Product development discussions. Every segment of our business increased contact with NCL. But in addition to function-specific discussions, I made sure we communicated our broader business needs consistently. Needs for specific new products. Needs regarding our digital infrastructure. I wanted to make sure that whenever NCL executives were meeting in Kyoto, they each had a consistent understanding of what made NOA tick and what would help us grow.

I also increased my direct communication with Mr. Iwata. Between my travel to Japan and Mr. Iwata's travel to the US, we saw each other monthly. Typically, we would have a series of group meetings with other leaders, and then Mr. Iwata and I would have numerous private meetings. These would focus both on near-term business issues as well as critical future needs. It was during these meetings that I pushed for controversial decisions, giving Mr. Iwata time to digest the issue before driving him to make a decision.

When Mr. Iwata or other NCL executives visited the US, we would often have team-oriented dinners in the evening. These would be great opportunities to better understand one another and share personal stories and experiences. But when I would visit Japan, I would very rarely meet with the most senior Nintendo executives for dinner. I believe this was because Mr. Iwata himself was a tireless worker, staying in the office until late at night meeting with members of his executive team. They often had simple meals brought in and continued discussing new game development projects well into the evening.

But on one of my first trips to Kyoto as NOA's new president, Mr. Iwata asked that I join him for dinner. This was a great honor; I knew Mr. Iwata rarely went out to dinner with subordinates. We went to the most prestigious restaurant in Kyoto. Food in Japan is presented with great artistry—visually beautiful and full of flavor. Typically, there would be six or seven small courses of exquisite food. That night, we had courses that ranged from sashimi, to Kyoto river fish and seasonal vegetables.

We shared stories about our childhoods. We laughed as we learned that each of us had read the entire family encyclopedia as young kids. For me, that was a twenty-six-volume *World Book Encyclopedia* set. We talked about our passions and the journey that had brought us together. "Reggie, you know we are very much alike."

"Mr. Iwata, what do you mean?" He was the world-class game developer and fourth-ever president of Nintendo. I was the brash marketer and disrupter.

"Reggie, Nintendo is a company where employees tend to stay for a very long time. But you and I are outsiders." Mr. Iwata had officially joined the company in 2000 before becoming president in 2002. "We have a unique challenge to understand and keep the company's culture while also pushing the company forward. I want you to really listen to all our employees. I want you to try to really understand their perspective before you begin to push your own ideas. You are very forceful. Our people, even NCL employees, want to please you. And you have very good ideas. But you won't always be right. Please make sure to think about the perspective of other people."

It was a profound conversation. He continued, "I have to do this, too. I am trying to push Nintendo in a new way. Yet Mr. Miyamoto and others have been part of the company for a very long time. I need to make sure they are with me as we go on this journey."

It was at the conclusion of this dinner that I felt we went from being in a boss/subordinate or mentor/protégé relationship to being friends. I would incorporate his insights into all my future work—at Nintendo and beyond.

THE SO WHAT

Leaders have to develop their self-awareness. As a leader, you've achieved success by pushing your ideas and challenging your team to outperform their individual capabilities. The best leaders have the ability to solicit input from others and build on this input. You can't be so enmeshed in your own ideas that you fail to incorporate the perspective of others.

LAUNCHING WII

One of the first key decisions in my new role as president of NOA would be launch planning for Wii. Despite a successful E3, Nintendo had not revealed all the launch details for the product. Launch date, price, games available on day one—all of these needed to be decided. We set the middle of September 2006 for our reveal, and I began negotiating the specifics with NCL executives.

Mr. Iwata and I quickly aligned on launching Wii in the Americas first. This strategy had worked well for Nintendo DS, and the Black Friday shopping occasion was a significant business driver in the Americas that did not exist in Japan or Europe. We also agreed that NOA would receive the largest initial allocation of the hardware.

But just as with the E3 presentation, we had a difficult conversation about how to best use *Wii Sports*. We knew we had something magical in *Wii Sports*. It perfectly highlighted how the Wii Remote could change game play and expand our customer base. The development team at NCL was adding elements that would give the game enough depth to satisfy the most passionate player. They also included different competitive elements that would encourage groups of people to play together.

I advocated packing *Wii Sports* with Wii so that every consumer would get access to this great content. After I made this suggestion, Mr. Iwata paused long enough for me to notice the faint buzz of the incandescent lighting in his office and get uncomfortable. "Reggie," Mr. Iwata said, "Nintendo does not give away precious content for free. We work hard to create special experiences. It is unique software that motivates consumers to buy our hardware. And we expect to sell these games over extended periods of time. No, we should not pack in *Wii Sports*."

"Mr. Iwata, I understand the value of our software. I know unique software has always differentiated Nintendo. But we know that Wii is a very different concept in the history of video games. Wii focuses on unique game play. The goal of Wii is to expand gaming from its current niche to a mass-market medium. *Wii Sports* has the power to do this. *Wii Sports* can be a unifying element for all players of the system and be a key motivation for people to buy the system and have fun immediately.

"Plus, Mr. Iwata, I know Nintendo has history using packed-in software to drive a system." I knew this from personal experience as I had bought my Super Nintendo Entertainment System in a bundle that included *Super Mario World*.

This was just the opening discussion on a topic that would last months. Even after convincing Mr. Iwata that this was the right approach, I would also need to get Mr. Miyamoto, as the head of all game development, to agree. I knew I was making progress when I was shown a new game on a trip to Kyoto in July 2006.

"Reggie, we understand your point about having a strong software title included with Wii during its launch," Mr. Miyamoto stated via a translator during a meeting with Mr. Iwata and Mike Fukuda. "Please take a look at this game that we are proposing to use for your idea instead of *Wii Sports*." The development team proceeded to show me an early version of *Wii Play*. This was a collection of different mini games that also showed off the capabilities of the Wii Remote. A number of the games had been shown earlier at E3 and had received further development.

The games were fun. One was a shooting experience; another was table tennis; and there was a neat game of billiards. But they lacked the thematic cohesiveness of *Wii Sports*. And the collection did not have a depth of experience that could lead to hours of play. They were the equivalent of cotton candy—fun for a moment, but not very filling.

"Mr. Miyamoto, these individual mini games are fun. I can see how the development teams have added more polish to the experiences we had earlier at E3. And they make excellent use of the Wii Remote," I said. "However, this doesn't feel to be the same complete experience that *Wii Sports* is. I don't feel including this would have the same impact as including *Wii Sports*.

"In fact, I have a different idea. Maybe instead of including this with Wii hardware, we should take this mini-game collection and include it with a Wii Remote to encourage additional sales of this accessory." The room was quiet for at least fifteen seconds.

Mike Fukuda jumped in, speaking in Japanese. I watched Mr. Iwata's and Mr. Miyamoto's faces and then heard the translation into English. "Reggie is right. *Wii Sports* does a much better job to achieve our objective of getting consumers to understand Wii immediately. And this mini-game collection is not a fully formed game that will command full price in our market. We should think about how to best use this software to achieve our objectives. Including this with the Wii Remote accessory is unconventional, but it would get more Wii Remotes in the hands of our consumers."

So now Mike and I were trying to get agreement to two different bundles, and the world's best game designer was not happy. The ever-present smile and impish squint of Mr. Miyamoto's eyes were gone. "Neither of you understands the challenges of creating software that people love to play. This is something we constantly push ourselves to do. We do not give away our software," Mr. Miyamoto stated.

Mr. Iwata, however, was already sparking to our ideas. "Miya-moto-san, I am sure that Fukuda-san and Reggie-san appreciate the effort of the developers. They are trying to solve for a different situation than ours in Japan." He went on to explain the market conditions we faced in the context of different game genres that performed well in the West versus Japan. He also explained how Micorsoft's Xbox 360 had just launched in 2005 and was doing well in Western markets. Clearly, our push to educate executives at NCL on our business needs was taking root.

We did not gain agreement during this meeting. Or the many others that followed. But we did eventually get Mr. Miyamoto and Mr. Iwata to agree to have *Wii Sports* packed in for all the Western markets. They decided to sell *Wii Sports* as stand-alone software in Japan.

This ended up being a perfect test of the different approaches. Wii broke records globally, but it performed the best in the Americas and Europe. It was in these markets that we had the phenomenon of *Wii Sports* competitions in bars, nursing homes, and on cruise ships. Including the software in the overall Wii proposition had been a courageous decision, and the right one.

Creating a bundle with *Wii Play* and a remote also was the right decision. This was sold globally—yes, even in Japan—and went on to be the fifth bestselling game in the history of Wii.

THE SO WHAT

Be willing to continuously make difficult decisions. Lean into these decisions, versus shirking them. Contemplate the issue from various angles before making that difficult call. But make it! And live with the consequences.

HAVING THE COURAGE OF YOUR CONVICTIONS

During the life span of Wii and Nintendo DS, there were many courageous decisions. For example, we decided to dramatically ramp up production for both systems in 2008 and 2009. Because of lead times, this decision had to be made a year in advance! Having the conviction to sell about twenty million units of each globally, two years in row, required deep business insight. And courage.

Another courageous decision was for NOA to provide Netflix capability in the Wii console. In 2009, as we were pushing this idea, Netflix was still early in its transition to a digital platform versus a disc-based DVD subscription business. Wii did not have DVD capability, so we were betting that a digital subscription effort would scale for Netflix. And this was essentially a North American initiative as Netflix was relatively small in Europe and almost nonexistent in Japan. NCL executives really didn't understand the business opportunity.

At this point, NOA had a reputation for not only courageous decision-making but also correct decision-making. With support from NCL, we announced that Netflix would come to the Wii console in January 2010. The inclusion of Netflix, plus the group game play of *Wii Sports*, positioned Wii to be the console of choice for the main living room television. By the holiday season that year, Wii was selling at the fastest pace in video game history.

Leaders have to make tough decisions all the time. That's because in well-run organizations, people are empowered and the easier decisions are made lower in the organization. It is the thorniest issue, with deep ramifications, that falls to leaders to decide.

Leaders don't have a crystal ball. They don't know in advance that the decision will work out. But they workshop the issue. They discuss it broadly and constantly to get alternative points of view. Then, finally, they make the decision and live with the consequences. Mr. Iwata's advice about seeking perspective and then making difficult decisions would be a lasting learning experience for me.

14

PIVOTING TO A SOLUTION

The video game industry is unique in that, to be successful, companies must maintain a near-constant pace of innovation. Typically, Nintendo of America would launch more than fifty new products a year: new games, new accessories, and new hardware variations. An incredible pace. Doing this successfully required a culture focused on delivering fresh proposals to constituents—constantly thinking about different ways to surprise and delight our consumers, our business partners, and our employees.

Video game hardware platforms such as Nintendo DS and Wii need to make a disruptive leap to the next generation every seven years or so. At the turn of the decade, in 2010, Nintendo was hard at work on their next innovations. The company needed something spectacular to succeed Nintendo DS as that platform had sold well more than a hundred million units by that time. Nintendo had considered many different consumer propositions and the technologies that would bring them to life.

LEVERAGING CONSUMER BEHAVIORS

As I engaged in discussion with developers, we coalesced around three core consumer behaviors that could lead to new game play innovations. First was the trend of the always-connected consumer. Initially driven by smartphone adoption, connectivity was migrating to all consumer devices because of accessible Wi-Fi. We envisioned delivering a variety of new experiences and updates to consumers as they physically passed by other owners of this new Nintendo handheld device, or when the owner connected to the internet. This dovetailed with our belief that consumers wanted new digital experiences to surprise them constantly.

Second, consumer desire was growing for direct download of their content to play anywhere and at any time. These could be big, fully featured games—AAA games in the industry vernacular—or they could be smaller, bite-sized games that were dominating mobile phone play. Our belief was that a Nintendo game shop providing all these different experiences would be a differentiator for us versus the current marketplaces offered by PlayStation, Xbox, Apple, or Google. And because our initial effort would be for the replacement of Nintendo DS, we would have the benefit of portability our home console competitors didn't have.

Third, we identified an emerging consumer desire for 3D video-based content. Movies in 3D had been in and out of movie theaters since the 1950s, but the early experiences were poor. In the 1980s, there were new experiences in big cinema franchises such as *Jaws* and *Friday the 13th*, but 3D felt like a bolt-on to the experience versus being a core element. All it did was produce an audience scream when the shark seemed to jump into your lap or blades appeared to come at your face. It wasn't until the commercial success of *Avatar* and the slick use of the new 3D glasses in cinemas that the technology really took root. By 2010, television manufacturers were selling 3D televisions, and more content was being made to take advantage of the technology.

Nintendo had a long and complicated history with 3D technology. In the early 1990s, Nintendo was experimenting with games that could be played in an immersive 3D world. These experiments were in two different directions: (1) traditional game console technologies and visual art styles that led to the launch of Nintendo 64; and (2) new stereoscopic optical technology that led to the launch of Virtual Boy in 1995.

Virtual Boy was an interesting but underdeveloped product. It sat on a tabletop, and players would place their foreheads against a hooded eyepiece to see red and black monochrome images. I had never played Virtual Boy until I was given a system as a gift. I don't know how the experience felt at the product's launch, but my relatively current experience felt crude. Only a handful of games were released for the system, and it was quickly abandoned as a commercial failure for Nintendo. Resources were redeployed into Nintendo 64 and the immersive open world 360-degree game play that system provided using 3D polygon visuals.

But the company never gave up on immersive 3D experiences. Nintendo experimented with a variety of technologies with the ultimate hope of providing true 3D visuals without the need for additional equipment or cumbersome glasses. The combination of LCD screen development, graphics processing speed, and chip sets capable of powering high-end game play and visuals came together in 2010. We announced Nintendo 3DS in March, and Mr. Iwata and I showed off the system at E3 in June 2010.

SEEING IS BELIEVING

Nintendo 3DS was a worthy successor to the bestselling portable console of all time. At E3, we ended the presentation by having more than 150 demonstrators move into the audience to show off the system and reinforce our positioning that "Seeing Is Believing" with Nintendo 3DS. It was a huge hit. We also showed off new games in the *Mario* and *Zelda* franchises, but the greatest enthusiasm was when we showed off games from the Nintendo 64 system that would be remastered in true 3D. One of the greatest games in video game history, *The Legend of Zelda: Ocarina of Time*, drove early excitement.

This was a joining together of the legacy side-by-side development of Virtual Boy and Nintendo 64—twenty years later.

I was excited about the augmented reality (AR) that we showed off with Nintendo 3DS. Technology pundits had always talked about the potential of virtual reality (VR). But to date, the content and experience have not delivered. Nintendo 3DS enabled AR game play via the two cameras on the back of the system, and we included AR experiences as part of the overall proposition. But most of all, it was fun and proved to us that there would be future AR opportunities. For example, *Pokémon Go* launched for iOS and Android devices globally in 2016 and has more than a billion downloads and more than 150 million active monthly users.

The combination of E3 and other announcements through fall 2010 built momentum for the launch of Nintendo 3DS. But it also led to a major disagreement between Mr. Iwata and me. During a December 2010 meeting, we reviewed the full slate of upcoming games. The information was disappointing. Nintendo would publish only two games at launch. Our development partners such as EA and Activision had only an additional fifteen games or so that would be available on the very first day of sale. This just wasn't enough to drive sustained sales momentum from the planned March 2011 launch until the holiday selling season. Also, the biggest game for the Western markets—*The Legend of Zelda: Ocarina of Time 3D*—would not be ready at launch.

THE PRICE OF INNOVATION

We shifted from discussing the software schedule to discussing pricing for the new system. "Mr. Iwata," I started, "we need to think about the entire proposition of Nintendo 3DS when we consider our launch price. While the 3D experiences we provide are fun and the potential of future experiences will also be great, because of the limited number of games at launch, I am concerned. I believe we need to be more aggressive with our pricing and launch in the US at $199."

"Reggie," Mr. Iwata exclaimed, "we have been discussing a higher price until now. You know this system is expensive to manufacture. And we need to be sensitive to the pricing for our current products in the market, Wii and DS. We need to focus on a higher price."

At the time, Wii was selling for $199 in the US, but we already recognized the need to get the price lower. Discussions were underway for a new Wii hardware variation that would reduce features like internet connectivity, but these were not interesting for my market. Wii, with all its existing capability, needed to be priced at $149 and eventually get to $99 to be the bestselling system of all time and dethrone PlayStation 2.

"Reggie, you know that it will be difficult for us to cost down Wii," Mr. Iwata said. "Even though we have sold more than eighty million Wiis, component costs for the system and the Wii Remote are still substantial. It is likely we will never get to the price points you want."

THE SO WHAT

Disruption takes many forms, including price-based disruption. Offering a unique bundle of benefits at an accessible price for a wide consumer demographic can upend a market. Bigfoot Pizza did this. A $99 fully featured Wii would have done this too.

SWING AND A MISS

Now was not the time to switch gears to discuss pricing for the existing systems. I learned that these discussions needed to be handled delicately and that the right timing was critical for achieving the desired outcome. In this discussion, I wanted to make sure we effectively launched Nintendo 3DS.

"Mr. Iwata, we can discuss pricing and overall plans for Wii another time. I want to make sure we launch 3DS the right way. We both know that Nintendo fans will buy our new systems at launch. They love our franchises and know that we always deliver great games. But we are facing increasing pressure due to smartphones and the experiences they deliver. And we are planning on launching the new 3DS games at a higher price than the previous DS generation. We need to consider all these elements. I want 3DS to be a long-term success, and I believe $199 at launch gives us the best chance to achieve this." I pressed hard.

"Reggie, we will announce all our launch details in a few weeks. Let me consider your points and discuss this with other Nintendo executives. We will talk about this again in early January 2011."

We reconvened in Kyoto after Christmas. "Reggie, I know you want to launch Nintendo 3DS at $199. But the economics for us at this price are impossible. You know we do not like to lose money on our hardware. Would you consider a launch price point like $219 or $229?"

These price points didn't make sense for markets in the West. Pricing is managed differently outside of Japan. In Western markets, companies can only suggest retail prices, not dictate them. In some European countries, manufacturers can't even discuss pricing with their retailers.

Also, in the West, retailers prefer price points above $100 that end in either $49 or $99. So a realistic price point for Nintendo 3DS was either $199 or $249.

Retail margins on hardware are typically slim—around 4 percent. So, even if we were to suggest $219 or $229, retailers instead were likely to price at $249 on their own and take a higher margin. This would create a missed opportunity to maximize our profitability and potential future problems as retailers would never want to revisit a 4 percent margin on next-generation Nintendo hardware.

Given these realities, I couldn't agree to Mr. Iwata's request. "No, Mr. Iwata, those alternatives do not make sense for us given the margin dynamics with our retailers. It needs to be either $199 or $249, and I continue to strongly recommend $199."

Mr. Iwata shook his head. "No, that is impossible. Then it will be $249."

With that, the decision was made and now my job was to execute the launch to the best of my ability.

THE SO WHAT

I think about decision-making and persuasive selling of disruptive ideas in terms of "batting average." I considered two statistics: good decisions versus bad decisions based on marketplace results, and gaining agreement for my ideas versus not gaining agreement.

Great leaders have a high batting average on both. I strove for .750 on decisions and .950 on selling ideas. Lofty goals that I didn't always reach.

But no one bats 1.000. Not every decision is the right one, and not every meeting ends in agreement to your idea.

I viewed my inability to convince leadership to price Nintendo 3DS at $199 at launch as my biggest failure while at Nintendo—to extend the baseball analogy, I struck out. But if you swing hard and with skill, you will have more hits than misses.

This would be one of the very few decisions Mr. Iwata and I would never align on. Some senior NCL executives failed to understand the overall dynamics of the Western markets—everything from the media landscape to the emerging ecommerce and omni-channel retail environments.

I redoubled my communication with senior Kyoto staff across all disciplines to enhance their understanding of the business outside Japan. And I pushed Mr. Iwata to add me to the global Nintendo executive management committee.

BRIDGING THE GAP

At the time, Nintendo operated with an old, Japanese-style governance structure. There was a board of directors made up of two or three representative directors of the company and two or three outside auditors. This group met relatively infrequently. The real decisions were made by the company's executive management committee. This group comprised Mr. Iwata, Mr. Miyamoto, the global CFO (Mr. Yoshihiro Mori during my initial tenure with the company, then Mr. Kimishima when he transferred from NOA to NCL in 2013), the head of global licensing and Japanese sales and marketing (Mr. Shinji Hatano), and the head of hardware research and development (Mr. Genyo Takeda).

This group met every other week to discuss both long- and short-term initiatives. There was deep historical knowledge about the games business and Nintendo's philosophy within this group. But there was little commercial knowledge for the Western markets. It was this group that had ultimately aligned on Nintendo 3DS's $249 launch price.

I pushed Mr. Iwata to bring a Western business perspective into this decision-making group. He understood the need but would always push back. While chairman for NOA, Mr. Kimishima would travel to NCL monthly to meet with the executive committee. He certainly was sharing the results of NOA's activity, but there was no question that I had more detailed knowledge about the key drivers of our performance, as well as deeper understanding of future potential issues and their solutions.

In the end, Mr. Iwata never put me on this executive management committee. But after his passing and when Mr. Kimishima became Nintendo's global president, he did change the structure to create a new group of executive officers for the company. I would be the first American named to this role.

THE SO WHAT

Effectively running a global business means understanding the complexities of all your key markets. No one person can do this alone. You need the benefit of leaders with deep local knowledge coupled with the leaders' curiosity about other regions and their business practices. This collection of globalists should make the effort to educate each other about their regions' distinctive business approaches and preferences. Then, seek common ground to get to the best global solutions whenever possible.

Nintendo 3DS launched in late February 2011 in Japan and late March 2011 in the Western markets. Preorders for the hardware were very strong, and the first few weeks of sales were exceptional. Globally, by the end of March 2011, more than 3.6 million units had been sold. This was the best performance at that time for any new system launch and especially meaningful since this was outside of a Christmas holiday peak season. But soon thereafter, we were already seeing a sales slowdown. As I predicted, the most loyal Nintendo fans rushed to the system, but the broader marketplace remained skeptical. The combination of high price and the lack of great software at launch was taking its toll.

A HUGE PIVOT

Mr. Iwata and I were having extensive conversations on next steps during April and May. We had strong software in our pipeline: *Legend of Zelda: Ocarina of Time 3D*, *Star Fox 64 3D*, *Super Mario 3D Land*, and *Mario Kart 7* from Nintendo, and new versions in the *Resident Evil*, *FIFA*, and *The Sims* franchises from our licensee partners. But a price decline would need to be part of our program. Once again, we discussed the issue.

"Mr. Iwata, I think a $50 price cut will be enough to spur momentum. I think we should execute this in the early fall as some of the new software launches. I believe I can keep our retailers supportive of Nintendo 3DS until then."

"Reggie, I know you will be able to hold the line with retailers in the Americas. Your team did a good job to manage their expectations and keep their inventory reasonable. But our situation is very difficult in our other markets. Retailers have bought significant inventory. They are pushing for us to accept inventory returns."

This would be a mess to execute. Ideally, you would only want full cases to be returned in such a program. But retailers would try to return every piece of inventory, including loose units. This would result in damaged product that we would not be able to resell at full price.

"Mr. Iwata, executing such a program would be a mistake. Even if this is just for one territory, it will cause problems throughout the global marketplace. This idea needs to be shut down."

"Reggie, to stop this push from retailers in the other markets we will need to move quickly, and decisively. We may need to be even more aggressive than your proposed $50 price cut."

"Mr. Iwata, we can be more aggressive, but it will affect our profitability globally. And if we move sooner with a price cut, we will need to create a program for our loyal fans who bought the hardware early. They cannot feel that we somehow misled them."

And so, we created a Nintendo 3DS Ambassador Plan providing the early buyers of the system the opportunity to download ten Nintendo Entertainment System games and ten Game Boy Advance games from our digital shop for free. And we executed a massive $90 price cut in the US, taking the system to $169. We made this move at the end of July 2011, just four months after launch.

This was a huge pivot. It cost Nintendo millions of dollars in profit. But it changed the long-term trajectory of Nintendo 3DS, and the system went on to massive sales beginning in the 2011 holidays. And we were able to manage fallout from retailers and fans from the price cut.

The entire experience reinforced for me the need to move decisively when faced with an issue or an opportunity. With 3DS, we did not let the poor sales performance linger. We moved quickly to create a plan and implemented it with excellence.

The episode also reinforced the need to consider fully the needs of your best and longest-term consumers. By implementing the Ambassador's Program, we kept our stongest fans engaged with Nintendo 3DS even when the price of the hardware was cut dramatically. They remained advocates for the system and used social media to post positive comments about the digital games we provided as rewards for their loyalty.

THE SO WHAT

No executive can be perfect with new initiatives. At one point or another, an idea will fail in the market.

Don't become overly cautious after a failure. As much as this may be a natural reaction, it is not a productive one.

Move forward with a willingness to take risks, to be aggressive, to disrupt.

15

SWITCHING THINGS UP

As we were working to address the nascent Nintendo 3DS, we were also working on plans for our next home console. Nintendo's Wii had shattered sales records during its first four years in the market. But now in its sixth year, sales had slowed dramatically. Typical tactics to spur sales had already been used—price cuts to $199 and $149, color variations in black and red—so we needed to work on the true successor to the platform.

THINKING ABOUT WHAT MIGHT BE, NOT WHAT IS

Nintendo's innovation mentality is rooted in defining new experiences that can delight the player but that cannot be achieved with existing hardware. This is different from the traditional competitors in the video game space who first consider technology, such as higher definition visuals and greater computing power.

We envisioned a new system that would seamlessly transition from game playing on a big screen television to playing on a handheld device. We knew that in most households a constant battle exists for the main screen in the living area. Our system would end these battles, as the game player would be able to just move their game from the large screen to the one in their hands.

We also saw the potential in having a touchscreen-enabled controller for players to toggle between game menus or quickly access items for the game. This would free up the larger television screen for the beautiful graphics of the game.

Lastly, we envisioned game play between the handheld screen and the larger television. Imagine flicking darts from the handheld screen to the dartboard shown on a television.

Nintendo developers were very excited by these possibilities. Developers from independent companies like EA and Ubisoft were also very excited.

We announced the new system, Wii U, in June 2011 at E3. Initial reaction was positive, but there was some confusion whether this was a true new system or just a new controller for the existing Wii. We defined the overall concept but didn't show real games that highlighted the system or its capabilities.

Nintendo fans discussed and debated these issues avidly for a full year until E3 2012. We were aware of this buzz and decided to communicate the benefits of Wii U aggressively. We created a globally streamed presentation that reached millions of consumers before the trade show even began. The content went deep into our approach and highlighted our quality-of-life features for the new system, including video chat and management of "all video content" from cable and streamers like Netflix and Amazon Instant Video. These were lessons learned from our experiences with Nintendo DS and Wii when we used *Blue Ocean Strategy* and *Innovator's Dilemma* to communicate our strategies.

During the actual E3 event itself, we highlighted all the great content coming to the Wii U system. Nintendo fan favorite franchises such as *Pikmin*, *Super Mario*, and *Legend of Zelda* were demoed or had breathtaking trailers shown. We also previewed fantastic content from our development partners. The following week, I was highlighting Wii U on *Late Night with Jimmy Fallon*. We were generating a huge amount of positive buzz.

The system launched just before Thanksgiving 2012. Once again, we had strong initial sales, selling about nine hundred thousand units in the US in the first six weeks of launch. But sales began to slow down early in 2013. The issue was the lack of available software that motivated players to buy the system immediately—meaning, while Wii U launched with twenty-three games in the US, no single game was "must have." They were fun . . . but did not drive immediate purchase of the system.

THE STRUGGLE

New versions of key software in the *Mario Kart* and *Legend of Zelda* franchises were not coming until 2014 or later. Coupled with the announcements that new Xbox and PlayStation consoles were launching during holiday 2013, Wii U sales struggled to gain momentum.

Once again, we were faced with a difficult situation that had to be addressed immediately. Wii U had launched with two versions: white with limited storage at $299 and black with four times the storage capacity at $349 including the game *Nintendo Land*, which we had featured during the 2012 E3 conference. We had hoped this game would be a system seller like *Wii Sports*, but it did not live up to our expectations. There was not enough volume to support the two different versions at retail, and the black bundle was outselling the white one dramatically, even with the higher price.

In the Americas, I took action to eliminate the white Wii U configuration and consolidate the volume on the black bundle. By summer 2013, we had taken the price of the black bundle down to $299. We also worked with NCL to create unique offerings for our market that would appeal to our players. These included black hardware with *Zelda* graphic elements and the game *Legend of Zelda:*

The Wind Waker HD and a different special hardware bundle that included *New Super Mario Bros. U* and bonus content called *New Super Luigi U.*

Promotions offering unique hardware and different software bundles are typical in the video game industry. But having to resort to these tactics within one year of launch was unheard of. It was clear that there were not enough product and pricing tactics to keep Wii U alive for a traditional five-plus-year life cycle.

THE SO WHAT

Businesses in trouble need immediate and decisive action. You don't have the luxury of time as the situation worsens around you.

Stay true to your principles and the key foundations of the business. Stabilize the situation, then prepare for the next wave of innovation to grow the business back.

NEXT-LEVEL PROBLEM-SOLVING

My attention focused on two areas. At NOA, we worked to keep retailers engaged with Wii U. There were still significant software launches planned including Nintendo's first multiplayer-focused shooting-style game called *Splatoon.* This title was strategically critical as it leveraged our work on a digital network platform enabling players to compete with each other across the globe. The game would also tap into the huge shooter category in the West. But the game was uniquely Nintendo. Instead of shooting bullets, players shot colorful blobs of ink. And the objective of the game was to cover more ground with your team's ink versus simply attacking your opponents. We had visions that this would be a great new franchise for the company and bring us squarely into the world of esports. I successfully lobbied Mr. Iwata and Mr. Kimishima for more marketing funds to support this launch, and it worked to drive sales and establish the franchise in the West.

The second area of focus was to clearly diagnose the problems with Wii U and apply these learnings to our next home console launch, which would need to come very soon. A few of the issues were clearly observable. The Nintendo-developed games were not launching on their original schedule. These delays meant we had huge gaps in new content for the Wii U buyers. A truism in the business was that you buy hardware for access to the unique games available. We weren't launching great games at an acceptable pace.

Tied to this issue was the lack of content coming from independent developers to fill in our own schedule. The issue here was our development tools. Because Nintendo had historically relied on internally developed tools to maintain the secrecy of our hardware innovation pipeline, the company rarely executed agreements with external tool providers. But the industry had changed. Now there were critical development tool companies such as Unity and Unreal Engine who created best-in-class technology. They were constantly updating these tools, which would help mask the timing for Nintendo's innovation pipeline. And these tools were used by thousands of developers—big and small—which could assure a steady pace of content coming to a system. We had to change our approach and incorporate these tools into the development architecture of our future systems.

There was a key positive element from the launch of Wii U. Players told us they loved the ability to play games both on their big-screen television and then transition to playing their game only on the Wii U game pad. But the game pad needed to be within twenty to thirty feet of the Wii U console and with no physical barriers between the game pad and the console so the wireless connection would work. Once consumers were too far away or obstructed, the game pad would lose its connection, frustrating the player.

MAKING THE SWITCH

This key insight would drive development of Nintendo's next system, code-named NX. We would provide a hybrid console that could deliver a beautiful experience on the player's large-screen TV and then be completely portable. This addressed a key player need—not having to stop your adventuring when you needed to leave your house to go to work or go to school. During a development meeting, I communicated this to the Kyoto team as the ability to play anywhere and anytime. This became the core positioning for NX.

During 2014 and 2015, I had numerous meetings with Mr. Iwata and the team of developers in charge of NX. Beyond agreeing to the positioning, we also agreed on the product name—Nintendo Switch—communicating the ability to "switch" from large TV-docked mode to portable handheld mode. We also made the difficult decision to delay a key game—*The Legend of Zelda: Breath of the Wild*—so that it could launch on both Wii U and Nintendo Switch.

While Mr. Iwata would pass away in the middle of the key product planning for Nintendo Switch, the system bore many of his touches. An intuitive user interface. Unique controllers called Joy-Cons that could be detatched from the main system. A robust digital shop enabling players access to a rich library of games.

The system launched in March 2017. In the months preceeding the launch, we executed a number of critical tactics to create excitement for the system, including a product trailer in October 2016 and my unveiling the system on *The Tonight Show* and letting Jimmy Fallon be the first non-Nintendo person to play *Legend of Zelda: Breath of the Wild*. To drive anticipation, we even ran a commercial in the Super Bowl before the system was available.

Everything about the launch was perfectly executed. We priced the system right at $299. We were clear in the key positioning and had a strong flow of software to motivate purchases. We exceeded our first sales goal for the system by 50 percent, and by the end of its first full year of availability, Nintendo Switch had sold more than fifteen million units—eclipsing the six-year sales total for Wii U. At the time of writing this, Nintendo Switch continues to be the fastest-selling system in video game history.

THE SO WHAT

Executional excellence doesn't get enough attention. The best ideas will suffer if they are not executed well. Preach the value of executional excellence and hold the organization accountable for it.

PUTTING SUCCESS INTO PERSPECTIVE

While the results were gratifying, the more important lessons were resilience and the necessity of strategic focus. From 2013 through 2017, Nintendo faced many challenges. We had the slow initial results of Nintendo 3DS and the need to turn around this critical part of our business. While smart devices and digital storefronts thrived, Nintendo needed to maintain relevance. The company decided to enter the mobile gaming business and launched a variety of applications with a mix of consumer and commercial success.

We had the struggles of Wii U and the need to fail forward by leveraging key elements that worked for the system into our next generation console, the Nintendo Switch. We made sure the system offered great value to consumers and that there was a steady flow of new games for players to own. Innovative companies and individuals must be resilient to overcome the inevitable failure that comes with taking risks.

Successful companies must also understand their historical equity and strategically leverage this equity in times of crisis. Nintendo's strategic equity is driving new game-play styles—from the mantra of bringing arcade-style capability into the home with the original Nintendo Entertainment System, to the motion-gaming of the Wii. The anywhere/anytime capability of the Nintendo Switch was a continuation of this strategic focus.

It was important to me to absorb these business lessons. I was starting to feel that Nintendo was now on solid ground. Nintendo Switch hardware was selling incredibly well, and the software sales were even better. *Legend of Zelda: Breath of the Wild*, *Super Mario Odyssey*, *Mario Kart 8 Deluxe*, and *Super Smash Bros. Ultimate* were all multimillion-unit sellers. And with the adoption of the third-party development tools I had advocated for, Nintendo Switch was home to innovative software from independent developers as well.

With the passing of Mr. Iwata, however, I also learned personally that life was fleeting. It would soon be time for me to move forward and focus my energy differently, in the time I had left.

16

THE NEXT GENERATION

We were at a leadership team dinner in February 2019. At this point, I had implemented a yearlong cadence of strategic reviews and financial planning for NOA. Typically, I would make a trip to Japan in late January or early February to lock down the broad financial parameters for the company and our contribution to Nintendo Co., Ltd.'s overall performance in the upcoming fiscal year that would begin on April 1. With these financial parameters in place, I would hold a daylong meeting with my leadership team to align on NOA's key business priorities that would deliver our financial performance. We would always kick off this activity with a dinner the night before.

This dinner was to be special for a couple of reasons. First, Flip Morse was going to retire from NOA in two months, and this would be his last planning session with the team. His successor was already announced, and she would be joining the dinner and the next day's session.

While Flip and I had started our relationship awkwardly back during my recruitment lunch fifteen years earlier, he and I had gone on to partner on many transformative initiatives for NOA. Everything from our recruiting practices, our new employee onboarding, our behavioral compentencies that drove rewards and recognition, and our compensation structure had been improved during my partnership with Flip. We had enjoyed a wonderful ride together.

> **THE SO WHAT**
>
> Sometimes a business relationship can start off awkwardly.
> Keep investing time and energy to improve the relationship.
> Reserve judgment and continue to get to know your colleague.
> You can start off on the wrong foot and then create a valuable
> relationship over time.

But the second reason our dinner was to be special was that I would be formally announcing my intention to retire from the company. About half the participants were already aware. Flip and our new head of HR knew about my surprise announcement as we had worked on the new organizational structure that would be in place following my departure.

My direct replacement, Doug Bowser, was also aware. We had hired Doug about four years before to head up our sales organization. Beyond sharing the name of Mario's arch nemesis, Bowser, Doug had the perfect background for Nintendo. Doug had also started his business career at P&G, although he was on the sales side and we had not interacted during my time there. Just before Nintendo, Doug had spent more than eight years at Electronic Arts, one of the largest game developers and publishers in the industry. Doug had progressed rapidly at NOA, adding marketing responsibility in 2016.

"Team," I told the assembled group, "we have shared tremendous successes together. Nintendo Switch is breaking records. Software is selling at unheard-of levels. We are delivering strong profitability for global Nintendo, performing the best of any subsidiary on all of our key metrics. But even more importantly, our organization is strong. We have been able to promote from within and give employees more responsibility without having to hire from the outside at senior levels. This is why I have chosen this time to retire from the company."

Many people were shocked; some weren't able to hide their emotional responses. And my own eyes were beginning to well up a little. I had to press on.

"I know this is a shock. And before you ask, no, it isn't for any sort of health issue. The fact is that I have been thinking about this for some time. But for me to leave, I needed the business to be on solid footing."

At this, I looked squarely at Don James. Don himself had been promoted to EVP of Operations as the business transitioned from N64 to GameCube. During this time, NOA had changed senior leaders across the finance and sales/marketing disciplines as well. He knew firsthand the challenges of changing senior leadership when the business is struggling.

"And I needed the leadership team to be in place. Doug will be my successor. We all have seen how well Doug has led our sales and marketing teams. He has been spending quality time with key leaders at NCL too. He will continue building those relationships. I know he is the right person to hand over the keys to our part of the Mushroom Kingdom." I had to throw in a fun reference to *Super Mario* to lighten the mood. I could see others had glistening eyes.

"So, I will be retiring on the same date as Flip: April 15, 2019. We've worked on so many initiatives together; this will be the final one as we prepare the NOA organization for its next phase."

THE SO WHAT

Great leaders exit a role knowing that their group will continue to perform well even when they are gone. It is the ultimate step in creating a lasting legacy. They have done all the mentoring and succession planning they can to set the group up for success.

With this the toasts began. As did stories from my part of Nintendo of America's history, many of which I have recounted here. It was the right way to break the news, with entertaining tales of how we had worked together to create epic programs that changed the video game industry.

The real work would begin the next day as we continued to shape the communication planning. We knew that this news could not stay secret for very long. It wouldn't be malicious, but inevitably someone would slip and make a comment beyond the limited people who knew this confidential information. I decided we would announce my retirement and Doug's promotion within two weeks from that dinner. Once announced, we would hold a series of meetings with employees across our various locations in Washington State, California, and New York City. Doug and I would also hold calls with key business partners.

It needed to be clear that Doug would lead the business in his own way. He would not be my clone in either business approach or media accessibility. I had been NOA's president and COO during a critical time when Nintendo needed a strong and visible leader. My partnership with Satoru Iwata and Shigeru Miyamoto during internal and external meetings was legendary. Doug would lead in his own style and with his own substance. I needed all our constituents to understand this, and accept it.

The next two months were a blur. Doug and I ramped up our time together as I exposed him to the finance, technology, and product development areas that he had been less involved in during his prior sales and marketing role. I also spent considerable time with each member of my leadership team to assure them that the business would continue to be just fine.

THE SO WHAT

No two leaders are exactly alike, and so managing a leadership transition should take differences into consideration. The exiting leader needs to properly position the new one by setting clear expectations about differences in style or approach and by reinforcing that the strong results should be the same.

It is a very strategic process, coupled with personalized comments and advice for the inevitable situation in which someone asks, "What about me? How will I continue to grow without you here?"

During this time, I also received a surprise phone call from the president of Ringling College of Art and Design, Dr. Larry Thompson. My daughter was finishing up her senior year as an illustration major at the school, and I was initially concerned that something was wrong with her. "No, not at all," Larry said. "This is about you. I would like to formally invite you to deliver the commencement address at Ringling College this May."

"Larry, this is a great honor. Especially with my daughter graduating this year. I have come to the campus at least once every year and have been able to build a connection there. I know so many of her friends; I am sure it would be a blast for them and for me. But you need to know—come May I will no longer be president of Nintendo of America." I needed to make sure he wanted me and not my role or the connection to the company.

"Reggie, that is perfect! We would be honored to host you on your first public act in retirement! We want you, your empowering story, and your wisdom for our students." With that, my first activity in retirement was set.

I began to craft a worthy commencement address. During my last few years as president for NOA, I had reconnected with leaders at Cornell University to serve on the advisory boards for the undergraduate Dyson School of Applied Economics and Management (my old stomping ground) and the communications department (which aligned with my current role in the gaming and media industry).

During my visits back to the campus, I would meet with students and share my personal story and the principles I live by. Their reactions reinforced the valuable lessons I had gained not just about leadership but about life as I moved from the Bronx to Cornell, from P&G to Nintendo. They were astonished that I had faced obstacles and setbacks as everyone faces, but I had persevered and overcome them all.

So, unlike business leaders who deliver a commencement built on platitudes and old sayings, I decided to craft the Ringling commencement around my five Life Principles:

1. What happens to you is up to you. I found so many young people abdicating parts of their lives to other people: their parents, their teachers, other adults, and advisors. I believe you need to own your journey, just as I owned my process to attend Cornell and my business journey that followed.

2. Life is hard, so dig deep. Even someone like me who is externally successful has faced exceptionally hard times. Tenacity and grit are essential qualities for everyone.

3. Be open to alternatives. My life would have been very different if I hadn't taken the risk of joining P&G versus pursuing banking. Or if I had listened to those people who told me not to join Nintendo.

4. Embrace your fear. Learning to be an effective public speaker was certainly one of my fears to overcome. Without this capability,

I would have missed out on so many business and personal opportunities.

5. Live in the moment and have some fun along the way. My passion for scuba diving and finding other ways to relax and rejuvenate from the stresses of life have been critical to my ability to achieve.

I worked on this address with the same passion as I did any of my past business presentations. I even had Don Varyu, himself now retired, look it over, and we wordsmithed it as we did in the old days. It was a fitting way to kick off my retirement.

I had received sage advice when I first started thinking about retirement from my physician, of all people: "Reggie, you are not the type to sit back and do nothing in retirement. Figure out what you love to do, and find ways to do it with people and institutions you enjoy working with."

THE SO WHAT

Every project needs to start with a vision. This means painting a picture for what you want to achieve. It must be clear. It should be captured in a collection of words or in a visual. It needs to be compelling, motivating all who hear it. There are some days when moving forward toward the vision is difficult. You will want to look at your vision statement to refocus and reenergize yourself toward the goal.

And just as I had done for brands and businesses throughout my career, I thought about the vision for my retirement. I realized that I loved helping people grow and businesses scale. From my earliest experiences as a people manager, I always felt the greatest enjoyment when I helped people thrive. And I knew that I loved growing businesses and overcoming complex challenges. Now I would look to find ways to do this in retirement.

I created my vision statement: to inspire and empower the next generation of leaders. I would achieve this through both direct one-to-one interactions, as well as larger interactions such as public speeches—and with this book. I would find ways to give back to communities and businesses that I valued, with the hope that I could shape the leaders and companies of tomorrow.

At just about the same time as I was organizing these thoughts, Cornell's Dyson School approached me with a unique opportunity. The school had been considering the creation of a Leader in Residence program where a business executive would commit to spend time on campus over a full academic year to interact with students, faculty, and administrators across a range of classroom instruction and campus-wide lectures. It would get me back to the Ithaca campus two or three times a year for a week at a time to share my leadership lessons and principles.

I jumped at this opportunity. This would be the ultimate "pay-it-forward" for an institution that was foundational to my adult journey. During my first visit in the Leader in Residence role, I gave a campus-wide lecture on my leadership principles, complete with many of the stories I have told here about setting grand visions and being courageous in decision-making. The lecture was held at one of the largest venues on campus. I warned the staff to be prepared, anticipating that attendees would likely queue up for questions and selfies when I concluded my talk. At first they minimized the issue, but as we came closer to the date and the event was at over-capacity, campus security became more concerned.

After delivering a presentation on my Principles for Next Generation Leadership, we structured the end of the event to have about thirty minutes of Q&A with attendees lining up at two microphones in the hall. True to my prediction, there was a mad rush to queue up, with a range of questions on my personal life, my time with Nintendo, and current political issues. The Q&A session was lively and ran long.

Afterward, an area was set up where attendees queued to have a brief conversation or selfie with me. This lasted almost two hours, even with group photos being taken to move the line along. It was both exhausting and incredibly fulfilling.

Another unique opportunity presented itself to me. Acclaimed journalist and author Harold Goldberg had created a special non-profit using video games as the medium to help young people develop writing, critical thinking, and communications skills within underserved communities around New York City. I had joined him for one session in late 2018 at the Dreamyard Preparatory Academy, a public high school with a focus on the arts that sits less than three miles from the Bronx tenement building I grew up in.

I had delivered one simple message to these students during this visit: I was you, and you can be me. I had grown up in a lower middle-class environment. But a focus on achievement had helped to set me on a path to success. Whether it was scholastic, athletic, or career achievement, grit and determination were key elements to my journey.

I also told them that both capability and opportunity need to be present to achieve success. Capability was created by their hard work at school, at home, or in the part-time jobs that many had to help their families financially. Opportunity was that moment when you stepped forward to apply these skills to achieve something significant.

While the students focused on every word I said, I was actually more motivated by their own stories. They were succeeding despite difficult situations at home and in their neighborhoods. I knew I wanted to get more involved.

Harold had been one of my early calls to talk about my retirement. Over the many interviews he had conducted with me at gaming industry events and the trip to Dreamyard, we had grown close. "Reggie," he said, "why don't you get more involved with my nonprofit? You've seen the work we do. And I have seen the look on the faces of students as they hear you speak. You're an inspiration to these kids."

Thinking back, I realized that, except for my parents, I had no real mentors before attending Cornell. I never benefited from hearing someone explain how to overcome challenges or share their insights for making big dreams become reality. Doing this for young adults in the Bronx and Lower Manhattan was a perfect role for me. Joining the New York Videogame Critics Circle became my first board position in retirement.

There would be other "full circle" moments for me. The woman I had hired at P&G who broke the mold for brand management and had gone on to a long and successful career there—Dina Howell—introduced me to the founders of the toy company Spin Master. This company reminded me of Nintendo: highly creative and innovative but in the middle of their transition to executional excellence. The company had key brands such as Paw Patrol and Bakugan, and they were creating new brands in the filmed entertainment and digital game spaces. Their need to succesfully grow beyond their current $1.5 billion in revenue fit perfectly with my capabilities and experiences.

I joined the Spin Master and GameStop boards just after I reached my one-year retirement anniversary. At the same time, the COVID-19 pandemic was beginning to close businesses and schools. I had been scheduled to be a keynote speaker at South by Southwest in March 2020, but unfortunately the event was canceled. Board meetings shifted to virtual mode but also dramatically increased in frequency as company management worked to keep the businesses moving forward and their employees safe.

I shared perspective from the business challenges I had faced, but this pandemic was completely different. We were all learning as we dealt with the day-to-day challenges.

The key point I reiterated at every call or videoconference was the need to be true to principles in managing the business and dealing with difficult issues. Protecting our frontline workers and enabling our office employees to effectively work from home were paramount concerns. Doing what was right, especially as the rules for limiting transmission of the virus were constantly changing, was key.

EPILOGUE

Endings can be challenging, both in careers and in books. How do you sum up so many experiences in a way that they're memorable and useful? I want to leave you with something that achieves both goals, but what?

It struck me that I have two simple messages. First, learn from the people who matter most during the course of a career. Importantly, you can learn from them while you're on the job and even later when they're no longer physically present.

Second, once a disrupter, always a disrupter. Even though I'm no longer at Nintendo, I still intend to pursue opportunities to disrupt—it's what gets my blood flowing and creates value for me, and I hope for others as well.

Let me share with you a few last stories that illustrate both points.

LEARNING FROM THE BEST

In writing this book, I have addressed a number of key relationships during my career. Two deserve more explanation and appreciation than I was able to offer during the narrative.

First is my relationship with Satoru Iwata. As I described a number of pivotal meetings with my friend and mentor, I focused on situations where we had some conflict or disagreement. These were inherently dramatic moments, but they were the exception rather than the rule.

The fact is, we were much more often in agreement and building on each other's ideas than arguing. I was fortunate that Mr. Iwata shared his ideas with me early and often, allowing me to provide input and Western perspective. In public meetings, he would compliment my thinking and opinions, a rarity in Japanese business management. Mr. Iwata would invite me to meetings held at Nintendo's European subsidiary, and then ask my opinion about their performance and future plans. I was proud to support him and be part of the gaming industry disruption and superior business performance that Nintendo delivered globally under his tenure.

Second is my relationship with Shigeru Miyamoto. This one was much more formal, but punctuated with moments of insight into his creative genius.

The majority of my time with Mr. Miyamoto was spent in Kyoto during group strategy sessions or product reviews. During these meetings, he typically did not ask many questions. Instead, he would be writing and sketching in a small, leather-bound journal. I sat with him during a lunch break early in my Nintendo tenure and asked him what he was writing in the journal.

"Reggie-san, I capture ideas. I am always thinking about new ideas."

I saw this process again many years later when Mr. Miyamoto was in New York City for a launch event. Mr. Minagawa, my PR and communications friend, was with him. Per our usual custom when he was in the US, Mr. Minagawa and I went for a drink after dinner. I knew he loved scotch and had made a reservation at Keens Steakhouse, one of the oldest restaurants in the city with a world-class scotch and wine list.

Just before we were to meet in the hotel lobby, Mr. Minagawa phoned me. "Reggie, is it okay if Mr. Miyamoto joins us?"

"Of course. I would enjoy spending time with him. But I know Mr. Miyamoto does not drink alcohol. What will he do as we are enjoying our nightcap?"

"Reggie, Mr. Miyamoto just wants to spend some casual time with you. And you know he loves coffee. As long as they have a fresh pot, he will be fine."

We were seated, Mr. Miyamoto with black coffee, Mr. Minagawa with a fine thirty-year-old scotch, and me with a nice red Bordeaux. Mr. Minagawa was at the center of the conversation, translating Mr. Miyamoto's comments into English for me and helping Mr. Miyamoto (who understands English reasonably well) grasp complicated English words or concepts.

I noticed that Mr. Miyamoto was constantly looking at the ceiling of the restaurant. He had noticed the thousands of thin-stemmed, churchwarden smoking pipes that lined it.

"Reggie-san, what is the story about all these pipes?"

I knew a little seventeenth- and eighteenth-century history, and understood that patrons would store their pipes at the local pub or inn. These clay pipes were incredibly fragile, so they were transported only once to Keens and kept there for safety. Patrons would light up their pipes after a meal. I shared my understanding with Mr. Miyamoto, but it wasn't sufficient. "I need to know more about this," he said.

I called our server over and had her explain more about the smoking pipes. But her explanation didn't provide much more detail than mine. We proceeded to pull more employees over. First was the headwaiter; next the front manager; finally, the most senior manager gave Mr. Miyamoto detail about a Pipe Club whose members included such luminaries as Teddy Roosevelt, Babe Ruth, and General Douglas MacArthur. And he shared names of more current celebrities who had pipes stored at the restaurant.

During all of this, I focused on Mr. Miyamoto. He was smiling throughout the translations by Mr. Minagawa as he heard this story. He would tilt his head and gaze at the pipes on the ceiling. I was imagining all the ideas that were churning inside Mr. Miyamoto's brain. If you next see a game from Nintendo that features a room with long, thin-stemmed smoking pipes on the ceiling, you will know where the idea came from.

I am fortunate to have partnered with him and Mr. Iwata, learning from two of the most creative and innovative minds in the gaming industry.

SAYING "NO"

Even in retirement from Nintendo, I continue to learn lessons and find ways to disrupt. After a tumultuous year on the board of GameStop, I decided not to stand for reelection. I joined that company's board because I saw opportunity to help this Fortune 500 company regain its footing and reinvent itself. Wall Street was betting otherwise.

Large hedge funds were "shorting" the stock, essentially taking a financial position that the stock price would go down, rather than up. As I talked to the GameStop CEO and other board members before joining the board in April 2020, the stock price was below $5 per share and the financial markets believed the company would be bankrupt before the new systems from PlayStation and Xbox were launched later that year. With the onset of COVID-19 that spring, the downward pressure intensified.

Behind the scenes and with guidance from the board, GameStop's management were making all the right moves. They were successfully negotiating with landlords for concessions on their leases as stores were closed or operating only limited hours. They were investing in their ecommerce capabilities so that they could serve customers whether they wanted to buy product in store or through the company's website. And management was negotiating with vendors to get the critical merchandise they would need to have a strong holiday selling season.

As GameStop navigated through the pandemic and paid off some debt, the stock price more than doubled through the fall of 2020.

One investor saw even more opportunity. Ryan Cohen, cofounder of Chewy, the successful ecommerce pet-supplies store, had amassed a near 10 percent ownership position in the company. Ryan had actually been approached to join GameStop's board the year before I joined. He had declined, but clearly the company interested him.

Ryan publicized a letter he had sent to the board in November 2020 demanding many of the changes that were already underway. Rather than have a bruising public fight with a major shareholder, the company nominated Ryan and two other former Chewy executives to the board, and they joined in January 2021. The announced plan was for a smaller slate of board members to be presented to shareholders later in June. I was on that initial slate.

But before I would fully commit, I forced a series of interactions with the new board members. I wanted to understand them, their background, and their plan. At the heart was understanding whether they were looking for a partner with strategic insight and disruptive ideas, or just someone to rubber-stamp their own ideas.

A new Strategic Planning and Capital Allocation Committee within the board was under discussion. This group would be responsible for a deep strategic review of all potential options for the company. I asked to be on the committee and be tasked with identifying the plans to transform GameStop. It made sense; I had the deepest industry knowledge on the board. I had ideas on how to provide GameStop customers with value beyond what they could get by simply downloading software from platform-holders like PlayStation and Nintendo. I had done business with GameStop as a vendor and as a customer, and I could speak to both the pain points and opportunity areas.

I was rebuffed. The response was that they wanted to keep this committee small. There was a desire to move fast; I understood this as not wanting anyone to challenge their direction.

Warning bells went off for me. Chewy was a $1 billion company when it was sold to PetSmart. GameStop was a $5 billion company and was already doing nearly $1 billion in revenue through its website. Completely different categories . . . completely different market dynamics.

Added to this was the difference in corporate governance. Chewy was a privately held company when Ryan ran it. He could do whatever he wanted. GameStop had shareholders to account to, and governance rules to adhere to.

It was shortly after these conversations when I informed Ryan that I would not seek reelection. In fact, all the independent board members—with the exception of the other former Chewy guys—decided to exit the board.

THE SO WHAT

Disrupt with integrity. In every situation, whether on a board or in a leadership position, the challenge is to shake things up while adhering to core principles. If you can't do both, then you have to leave and live to disrupt another day.

THE GAME CONTINUES

I continue to stay involved in the games business as an advisor and an investor. With so many friends and past business acquaintances in the industry, I get to see ideas early in development. Now, I am the mentor to these young executives looking to disrupt the industry with a breakthrough idea.

I have been fortunate to get involved in a variety of new creative projects. The most exciting is a documentary within the broad video game space in partnership with Harold Goldberg, founder of the New York Videogame Critics Circle, and Ryan Silbert, Academy Award–winning producer and fellow alum from Cornell University. Creating content is a long and winding road, so I won't share much more about the concept or the expected timing. But I am excited about the possibility of working on film and podcast initiatives that will help me further my mission of inspiring and empowering the next generation.

Board service and my creative projects have given me ample time to think about the increasing value of disruption. Our world is constantly changing—whether you look through the prism of business, climate, politics, or social justice. Yet the solutions being offered suffer from sameness and reliance on an old, tired playbook.

In addition to relying on the old approaches that put us in this difficult situation, people are scared to take risks. They are leery of offending by pushing too hard, or suggesting a completely alternate path. They don't want to be "canceled."

We live and work at a time when we are facing huge, complex problems. Solutions won't come from traditional thinking or being terrified of doing something different. You need to disrupt the game. Disruption drives innovative thinking and more effective problem-solving.

Select the right topics in your own orbit and be aggressive with new thinking and new approaches. Drive change. Disrupt the game.

ACKNOWLEDGMENTS

I have been blessed to have had many coaches, mentors, and sponsors throughout my journey.

My parents were my first coaches. They taught me right from wrong and the fundamental value of principles. Unfortunately, my father passed away early in the writing of this book. My mother enjoyed sharing old photos and confirming details to help me in the retelling of family stories. In turn, she was surprised by all the new stories she learned about me.

During my school days, I was fortunate to have a core group of key friends. Over the past few years, I have been able to reconnect with four of my best friends from that time, and we have dubbed ourselves the Brentwood Five. Each of them has had a great career and family life, and when we see one another we fall into a wonderful balance of old times and new experiences. These guys have done a great job keeping me grounded during the development of this manuscript.

Just as with my Brentwood friends, my friends from Cornell, my fraternity brothers in the Gamma Chapter of Phi Sigma Kappa, and my colleagues from every step in my career have helped me grow. This is especially true of all my friends and associates during my tenure with Nintendo, who are too numerous to mention individually. Thank you for your friendship and support.

Throughout the book, I have called out key mentors who helped me in my journey. Professors Aplin and Anderson at Cornell University. Bob Gill at P&G. Gary Matthews at Guinness and Derby Cycle.

John Sykes at VH1. Satoru Iwata at Nintendo. Each was invaluable in shaping me as a business executive and as a person.

This book would not have happened if Fred Cook, chairman emeritus of Golin, Nintendo of America's public relations agency, had not visited Stacey and me shortly after my retirement. Over dinner, we talked about his book—*Improvise*—and he told me I should write my own. He proceeded to introduce me to Bruce Wexler, a publishing industry expert who has been involved in numerous bestselling books across a variety of genres. Bruce proceeded to read every proposal, chapter, and edit of this manuscript. He made this book better at every opportunity.

Sara Kendrick, Ron Huizinga, Sicily Axton, and the entire team at HarperCollins Leadership worked tirelessly to help this novice author navigate the challenges of publishing a book during a pandemic and a supply-chain crisis. Thank you for making this a great experience despite all the challenges.

Howard Yoon, Barbara Hendricks, and Nina Nocciolino were huge assets in driving the project forward despite my constant questions and suggestions to explore alternative approaches.

A very special thank you to my best proofreaders: my wife, Stacey, who read every iteration of the manuscript, sharing ideas and edits, and her sister, Amy Luce, who generously lent her time and grammatical expertise to make sure we got it right. Anything that is inconsistent with *The Chicago Manual of Style* is my fault.

In addition to the individuals named in the book, my special thanks to: Jennifer Archer, Alison Holt Brummelkamp, Jimmy Fallon, Rick Flamm, Carrie Bergstrom-Halls, Ken Calwell, George Harrison, Jim Henderson, Brandon Hill, Stephen Jones, Dave Kass, Geoff Keighley, Mark Keller, Rick Lessley, Dom Maiolo, Chip Martella, P. J. McNealy, Anna Nero, Bruce Raines, Arjun Sen, Kevin Sherry, Ryan Silbert, Steve Singer, Jacqualee Story, Leslie Swan,

Liane Ramirez-Swierk, Andrew Swinand, Eileen Tanner, Rob Thompson, Kristie Tomkins, and Lisa Zlotnick.

Lastly, I wish to thank you, the reader, and all those who continue to connect with me at events and online. I hope you have found my stories and insights useful in your own journey to disrupt the status quo.

INDEX

ABOUT THE AUTHOR

REGGIE FILS-AIMÉ is an award-winning innovator and disrupter most recognized as the former president and chief operating officer of Nintendo of America, the largest division of the Japanese entertainment company Nintendo Co., Ltd. In this capacity, he helped bring the Nintendo DS, the Wii, the Nintendo 3DS, the Wii U, and the Nintendo Switch to the global marketplace.

Reggie joined Nintendo of America in December 2003 as executive vice president of sales and marketing. In May 2006, he was promoted to president and chief operating officer. He ran the day-to-day operations of Nintendo of America and was responsible for all activities of Nintendo in the United States, Canada, and Latin America. In 2016, Reggie was appointed to the global Executive Officer Committee for Nintendo Co., Ltd. He retired in April 2019 and was inducted into the International Video Game Hall of Fame in October 2019.

Reggie graduated with distinction from Cornell's Dyson School, which launched a more than thirty-five year career spanning the consumer-packaged goods, restaurant, beverage, and media/entertainment industries.

Since retiring, Reggie has focused his energy on cultivating the next generation of business leaders. In August 2019, he was named the inaugural Dyson *Leader in Residence* for the 2019–2020 academic year. He is currently sharing his personal learning and principles through public speaking, board service, and *Disrupting the Game,* published by HarperCollins Leadership. Lastly, Reggie founded Brentwood Growth Partners to help emerging companies scale and enable leaders to create world-class cultures.